PUBS
IN AND AROUND THE
YORKSHIRE
DALES

PAUL CHRYSTAL

O Yorkshire, Yorkshire: Thy Ale is so strong
That it will kill us all if we stay long:
So they agreed a Journey for to make
Into the South, some Respit there to take.

(George Meriton 1684, *The Praise of Yorkshire Ale*)

The destroying hand of progress.

(T.P. Cooper, 1897, *The Old Inns and Inn Signs of York*)

The death knell for many a Dales pub, so often the victim of myopic, and often plain ignorant, council 'decision makers', even today.

And this from *AdoptaPub* regarding the Black Bull in Reeth:

Apparently the pub had featured this whitewashed front for many years, and the landlord decided it was time for a change, and faithfully restored the building to its original Yorkshire Dales stone. Looked lovely apparently. Then the National Parks got in on it and told him he had to put it back to the whitewash, even though almost all the villagers signed a petition agreeing that the natural Yorkshire Dales stone was much nicer.

The landlord could not win against the large and powerful Parks Board, and so re-whitewashed his pub. But he hung his sign upside down, so that anyone who walks into his pub of course will ask, 'Why is your sign hanging upside down?' and of course, he is only too willing to tell the whole story.

Apparently the Parks Board is something of a thorn in the side of a lot of the locals who are only trying to live there, but constantly have to battle a bunch of bureaucrats who want the Dales to look like DisneyDale.

(http://www.sunriseag.net/adoptapub/more/0030BlackBullReeth.htm)

First published 2018
Destinworld Publishing Ltd
www.destinworld.com

© Paul Chrystal 2018

All rights reserved. No part of this book may be reprinted or reproduced or utilised in any form or by any electronic, mechanical or other means, now known or hereafter invented, including photocopying and recording, or in any information storage or retrieval system, without the permission in writing from the Publishers.

British Library Cataloguing in Publication Data.
A catalogue record for this book is available from the British Library.

ISBN 978 1 9997175 9 9

Cover design by Ken Leeder

BY THE SAME AUTHOR

Hull Pubs

Harrogate Pubs (including Knaresborough)

Pubs In & Around York

The Place Names of Yorkshire, including pub names

Haworth Timelines

Old Yorkshire Country Life

Yorkshire Literary Landscapes

ABOUT THE AUTHOR

Paul Chrystal has Classics degrees from the Universities of Hull and Southampton; he was a medical publisher for nearly forty years and is the author of 100 or so books, many of which are about Yorkshire; this is his fourth pub book. Paul is a regular contributor to a number of history magazines, is a reviewer for 'Classics for All', writes for a national daily newspaper, has appeared on the BBC World Service, Radio 4's PM programme and various BBC local radio stations. He lives in York.

ACKNOWLEDGEMENTS

This book would have been impossible to write and complete without the friendliness and kindness showed, without exception, by the scores of licensees and their staff whom I visited during the course of what was an arduous research project. Cheers!

Thanks too to Kevin Avery for permission to use his Kilnsey Crag image. Patrick Turton, Bar 13 Settle; Colin Hinson, Neil Hinson, Jon Dawson and Tim Mason for the photographs by Lucie Hinson © Lucie Hinson; Mike Kenney, Tan Hill Inn; Eric Lucas and Ian Paradine at Daleside Brewery and Harper Creative Ltd for the sketches; Tom Fozard, Commercial Manager, Rooster's Brewing Co; Jonathan Shepherd, Wharfedale Brewery Limited; Timothy Taylor & Co. Ltd; Helen Crannage, Pennine Brewing Co; Rachel Stafford, Hambleton Ales; Geoff Southgate, Wensleydale Brewery Ltd; Black Sheep Breweries, Masham.

The hamlet of Booze in Arkengarthdale. Slei Gill looms in the background.
Photographer: Jamesfcarter

CONTENTS

OPENING TIME

I would give all of my fame for a pot of ale and safety.

(William Shakespeare, 1564–1616)

This is a practical beer (and soft) drinker's guide to the public houses in and around the Yorkshire Dales National Park. The book is 'practical' because the maps show you how to get there, I give addresses, post codes, phone numbers and websites (where they exist), and I point out anything special to look for once you're there. To make things easier for the reader, the book is organised by dale or region, as shown on those useful maps at the front of the book.

People come to the glorious Yorkshire Dales from all over the world for many reasons. They come here for the breathtaking scenery, the peaceful solitude, the buzzing market towns and villages, and for … the pubs. This book celebrates no fewer than 136 of those pubs with information, where available, on their history, anecdotes about them and about characters who may have drunk in them, and items of local interest associated with them. Given the number of pubs in the National Park and their popularity, it is astonishing that although there is a plethora of books on pub walks, no book until now exists on the pubs themselves. As well as offering a useful guide to pubs in the Yorkshire Dales, it also provides a pictorial history of the dales and of dales life through its pubs, inns and hostelries.

There is also a chapter on some of the breweries that serve the pubs of the Yorkshire Dales, which, if nothing else, evidences the rise and rise of the vibrant, innovative and exciting microbreweries in the region.

Context and balance are provided by a chapter on temperance. There is a chapter on intriguing, eccentric and daft pub names in Yorkshire and, finally, just as any good pub worth its hops has a programme of guest beers, so then shall this book feature a guest pub: a pub that is not actually in the Dales 'but that would grace any village, town or city with its unique atmosphere and ambience, exuding everything that is just right about an English pub'. The wonderful Hales Bar in Harrogate featured as the guest pub in my book on York pubs; this time it is the Old Bell Tavern, also in Harrogate – a fine stopping place for anyone coming to the Dales from the east or the south.

A word of caution: information is correct at time of going to press, but pubs are closing or being inflicted with a change of use all the time, so please do check the latest situation if setting out to visit.

To give some historical perspective – and to highlight the seemingly inexorable decline of pub culture – back in 2003 the average pub price per pint of draught bitter was £1.95.* Times have indeed changed since then: then, the average adult drank 218 pints per person; by 2011, that same adult downed just 152 pints, a 30 per cent drop.** In 2002 there were 60,100 pubs in the UK.*** There were 50,300 pubs at the end of 2016, down from 54,194 in December 2014, according to CAMRA.

Top of the world: Tan Hill Inn and *aurora borealis*

---

*   www.statista.com
**   telegraph.co.uk/finance/newsbysector/retailandconsumer/11283995/The-real-reasons-for-the-tragic-demise-of-the-British-pub-industry.html
*** www.beerandpub.com/statistics

INTRODUCTION

there is nothing that has yet been contrived by man, by which so much happiness is produced, as by a good tavern or inn.

(Samuel Johnson 1709–1784)

As I remarked in the introduction to the sister book on pubs in and around the city of York, in the days before Sat Nav, if you stopped and asked a stranger the way to somewhere, anywhere, you would most likely be directed by way of the local church (if there was one) or via the local pub or pubs. Generally speaking, pubs are still, despite all the closures, the second most ubiquitous feature of most high streets, be they urban or rural or suburban. That tells you just how important pubs are to any local community; like churches, they can be the focal point of a street, estate, village, town or city centre. Like churches they can, for some, satisfy a very real need for refuge, companionship, comfort and joy.

Pubs and their names, like the names of towns and villages, hills, fields, rivers and dales, often tell us much about local history in the vicinity, famous local people and local topography. This book gives a selection of some of the more interesting Dales pubs with a tale to tell; some are still with us, others are long gone – but those that are closed are often just as eloquent about the past as those whose doors remain open.

In 1875 Yorkshire as a whole could boast some 10,000 pubs. Now there are significantly fewer, with time being called for the last time all the time. The message I offered in my book on the pubs of Harrogate and Knaresborough is just as valid here:

> *So, if there is a message to take away from this book it is simply put the book down, get up, go out and call in at your local for a pint or two and help preserve and extend this most British of social institutions. Once the pub, your favourite pub, has gone, it's often gone for good.*

But don't take it from me – in the words of no less an authority than the ever-cautious Hilaire Belloc (1870–1953):

> *When you have lost your inns drown your empty selves for you will have lost the last of England.*

He's right. Ask any villager whose local has been erased from the face of his main street.

How did our pubs come about? In the beginning, pubs, particularly pubs out in the country, brewed their own ale in brewhouses next to the pub; women often did most of the work: Madam Bradley of Northallerton and Nanny Driffield of Easingwold are veritable legends in their own brewhouses; 'Brewsters', or 'alewives' brewed ale in the home for domestic consumption and commercial sale, albeit on a small scale. These brewsters made a substantial and vital contribution to the family income. It was good ale that attracted neighbours into their houses and eventually led to the birth of the public house.

Yorkshire's Stingo, Knockerdown and Rumtum were famous strong Yorkshire brews with well-earned reputations as far south as London's Marylebone. Stingo even had pubs named after it. Hopped ale was imported from Flanders around 1400, after which hops were home-grown in England for beer production: ale usually has a lower hop content than beer. At the same time, hostelries were set up by the roadside catering for travellers. This had started with the Persians and Hellenistic Greeks in the 2nd century BC and perfected by the Romans locating *tabernae* on their extensive road network to proffer wine to marching legions and various other travellers. Essentially, this *cursus publicus*, public way, was made up of thousands of posting stations along the major road systems of the empire where riders and travellers took food and refreshment and horses were watered, shoed, cared for by vets, stabled, and passed over to fresh dispatch riders. Later on vehicles were garaged here and the taverns provided for merchants, refugees, magistrates or court officials in transit between cities.

Catering on the hoof continued apace with merchants from the Middle Ages plying between markets, as well as long-distance drovers, commercial travellers, monks commuting from monastery to monastery, pilgrims (as exemplified by Chaucer's *Canterbury Tales*) and all manner of other people moving from village to village or from town to town. Lords of the manor sometimes provided refreshing and sustaining beer-house facilities for the thirsty workers toiling in their fields.

Ale was an important part of the Dalesman's diet, being as it was affordable, and unpolluted, unlike water. It is estimated that the average adult then drank up to eight pints a day. Taverns, though, got off to a bad start around the Dales when Ecgbert, Archbishop of York, around 735 AD declared ale houses to be off limits and decreed that 'no priest go to eat or drink in taverns'. Nevertheless, during King Alfred's reign (871–899) alehouses proliferated, identifiable by the ale stake – a long pole stuck outside along with a bush if wine was also on offer. In 997 AD alehouses, and their tendency to foster anti-social behaviour, entered the statute book when King Ethelred (979–1013) tried to put a price on drink-fuelled disorder with an edict that stated 'in the case of a breach of the peace in an alehouse 6 half marks shall be paid if a man is slain'. He introduced prohibition when he closed down many a tavern and restricted them to one per village. He was also the inadvertent inventor of the drinking game tradition when he introduced pegs in drinking horns – the drinker was not to go beyond the next peg with each draught. The 1215 *Magna Carta* had a go at establishing 'standard measures of wine and corn'. In 1267 the Assize of Ale and Bread was the first attempt, by Edward III, to establish the price of ale and minimise extortionate overpricing. It laid down conditions on brewers and ale wives, taverners and hostelers (innkeepers). From this we start to see a distinction between inns, taverns and alehouses: innkeepers provided accommodation for travellers; taverners bought wine from vintners (wine wholesalers) and resold it to their customers for consumption on their premises; ale brewers sold ale to alehouse keepers for resale in the alehouse. Licensees of ale houses were later described as tipplers and ale drapers.

In 1393 Richard II introduced more regulation when he saw the tax potential to be had in ale and decreed that 'whosoever shall brew in the town with the intention of selling it must hang out a sign'. In so doing he not only gave birth to the fine tradition of pub signage, he also made life easy for his revenue men and for law enforcers to spot potential tax and trouble. Hitherto, most early ale houses were located in private houses, so there was no need for regulation or the signage that went with it. Richard II's action also explains why many pub names have associations with the Wars of the Roses (1455–1487) – Rose & Crown, White Hart, Blue Boar, and so on; the decree came relatively soon before the start of the war, which will have provided a source of fresh, new names.

Thanks to their continued unsavoury reputation, alehouses later got sucked into 1496 legislation relating to 'vagabonds, idle and suspected persons' when justices of the peace gained powers to 'rejecte And put away common ale selling in townes and places where they shall think convenyent'. In 1552 keepers of alehouses and tippling houses were required to be licensed; tippling houses were places where beer could be sold but not brewed.

By the mid-16th century there were 19,759 taverns or inns in England and Wales, or 1:187 people compared with 1:650 today.

The Alehouses Act of 1551 was a central government attempt to deal with the 'abuses and disorders as are had and used in common ale houses'. Justices of the Peace could apply sanctions to rowdy establishments enabled as they were 'to remove, discharge and put away common selling of ale and beer'. The apparent problem with taverns was that that there was deemed to be too many of them and that the wine served was usually of dubious quality. So, in 1553 the number of taverns was restricted by law: London was allowed forty, York a mere eight and Hull and other comparable sized cities a miserable four. However, legislation so universally, yet gleefully, ignored and unenforced would be hard to find: in 1623 there were still 13,000 licensed premises in England.

In 1572 Elizabeth I's Council of the North, established in York, demanded yet more robust regulation; in 1604 legislation – An Act to Restrain the Inordinate Haunting and Tippling of Inns, Alehouses, and Other Drinking Places – was passed to redefine the very role of drinking establishments: they were definitely not for 'Entertainment and Harbouring lewd and idle People to spend and consume their Time in lewd and drunken Manner'. What they were for was the 'Receipt, Relief and Lodging of Wayfaring people from place to place'. Having fun, social cohesion and inculcating a community spirit then, were officially subsidiary to the provision of board and lodge.

Ironically, and awkwardly, things then became very confusing when tipplers were required by law to 'serve all the Queen's people, without refusal for their ready money'; trouble makers or not, they had to be served. In this blizzard of well-meaning but ineffective legislation, evasion was rife, especially illegal brewing and keeping an alehouse without a licence; the production of illicit ale was far too profitable for it not to be; the corollary to this was the effect of strong beer on the average temper and temperament, effects that were all too predictable. And so the bar room brawling continued. But it was by no means wall-to-wall violence: in the ongoing battle against illicit production and rowdiness some progress appears to have been made by 1743. New laws restricted the issuing of licences to keepers of public houses: only one licence could be held, licences could only be issued at Brewster Sessions and transfers at Transfer Sessions, licensees had to be of a higher social standing and were required to produce sureties of good behaviour.

Things started to change nationally in the 17th century when in 1657 turnpikes led to a huge increase in the number of horses and coaches full of passengers crisscrossing the country. The railways 200 years later brought the next seismic change with the establishment of railway inns at stations; a third development was the now ubiquitous motor car and the transportation of goods by road, all of which necessitated catering for day trippers, business people, long-distance lorry drivers and other travellers – often in the very pubs that once served coach and railway travellers.

The first common brewers were the Nesfield family of Scarborough established in 1691; the end of the 18th century saw the emergence of the common brewery; this was boosted by Wellington's Beerhouse Act of 1830 with names from the 19th century like Hull Brewery, John Smith's, Sam Smith's, Tetley's, Timothy Taylor's and Theakston's, most still very much alive in the 20th century and, in some cases, into this century. Beer brewing had moved out of the home and was an industry in its own right, supplying a growing number of public houses and hotels. The aim of the Beerhouse Act was to encourage people to drink beer rather than spirits, gin mainly. Any householder that paid the poor rate could sell beer, ale or porter by buying an excise licence; they did not a need a justices' licence but spirit selling retailers did. Sellers of ale had to promise to give correct measures, maintain good order, to allow no drunkenness or gambling, and not to dilute the beer! The Beerhouse Act abolished the beer tax, and extended the opening hours of licensed public houses, taverns and alehouses to from fifteen to eighteen hours a day.

The Act also gave rise to the beerhouses and beershops that were permitted to sell only beer. Opening hours could be from 4 a.m. to 10 p.m. – good for a breakfast pint. For 2 guineas payable to the local excise officer, anyone could now brew and sell beer. The excise licence would stipulate whether the beer could be consumed on the premises (beerhouse) or as off-sales only (beershop). Supervision by local justices was severely curtailed leading to complaints by magistrates and local gentry keen to control the working classes in their area.

Not everyone warmed to the Act, driving the making of beer underground and doing nothing for the fight against intoxication: many beerhouses emerged from the back streets of large cities and became working class drinking dens. *The Leeds Mercury* of 23 October 1830 reported, 'We receive from many quarters grievous complaints of the demoralising effects of this Act, which has, by making beer cheap, led to an increase of intoxication'. The Beerhouse Act of 1830 also saw licensed premises double in ten years with 24,000 new licences issued within three months of the legislation. It also galvanised the rise and rise of the common brewery, brewing beer and selling it to other outlets rather than brewing for oneself.

Beerhouses provided not just beer, but food, games and some even lodging. They were also known by the name 'small beer' or 'Tom and Jerry' shops. In villages and towns many shopkeepers opened their own beershop and sold beer alongside their usual wares. Beer would be brewed on the premises or purchased from brewers. Many beerhouses inevitably became the haunt of criminals and prostitutes, with some eliding into thinly disguised brothels. The official reaction was to raise the excise fee to 3 guineas and to introduce property qualifications. But only the Wine and Beer House Act of 1869 brought the licensing of the beerhouses back under the control of the local justices. Many then closed, or were purchased by breweries and changed to fully licensed public houses.

Pubs were never always just pubs. Many doubled up as coroners' and magistrates' courts, as markets, morgues and as smugglers' dens: smugglers always drank in the Ship in Saltburn; others were also blacksmith's, cobbler's or carpenter's – often the landlord's day job. The Denmark Arms in Scarborough was also a grocer's until its closure. Appropriately enough, The White Boar in Huddersfield was also a butcher's. Fiddling the customer has always happened: in 1734 the landlord here, John Walker, was fined for giving short measures. The Beaumont Arms at Kirkheaton near Huddersfield doubled as an undertaker's. The Three Nuns at Mirfield was where the local nuns brewed their own ale. The Cricket Inn in Sheffield's Hyde Park had its own cricket pitch from 1826, as has The Strafford Arms at Stainborough nearby. The Victoria Park Hotel in Sheffield had a bowling green and 'an American bowling alley' in the mid-1800s. The Crooked Billet at Ryhill near Hedon housed a slaughterhouse. Best of all, though, was The Humber Tavern in Paull east of Hull; here, in 1836 Trinity House decided that 'lights be exhibited in the windows of a public house at Paull as a temporary expedient until the erection of permanent lights'.

Pub signs and the names and the images depicted on them make an intriguing subject all of their own. The Romans started it all with a welcoming sign showing a bunch of vine leaves representing the wine god Bacchus to denote a *taberna* – the place for a legionary, government official, itinerant or a merchant to slake his thirst. As with any other commercial enterprise, pubs use signs or symbols to signify the nature of the business going on within. The barber's pole and the pawnbroker's balls still survive to this day: the reason for all this symbolism was that until the end of the 19th century most people could not read, so word signage would have been quite useless: a symbolic, graphic sign, however, clearly spoke volumes. For pubs, a garland on a pole, the ale-stake, denoted a place where drink could be had. Red lattices on glassless windows also gave the game away for what was on offer within. From 1393 it was a legal requirement for innkeepers to display a sign: pub owners accordingly invented names and signs to differentiate their pub from the one up the road: your sign set you apart from other inns and taverns in the locality; it might also advertise what might be found inside (for example, cold meats or board games as well as ale), or indeed the political leanings of the landlord and his clientele. Coats of arms reflect the custom adopted by noblemen in which they displayed their banners outside the inn to show that they might be found within. York's imposing gallows sign at Ye Olde Starre Inne spanning Stonegate is a very rare surviving example of these literally unmissable pub indicators.

The name Royal Oak indicated a supporter of Charles II (he hid in an oak at Boscobel after the battle of Worcester in 1651 before restoring the monarchy in 1660); Punch Bowl denoted a Whig establishment and their patrons' predilection for punch. The Tories still preferred port and red wines. Marquis of Granby reflected the philanthropy of said Marquis to his veterans. Chequers denoted board games available while The Board proclaimed that cold meats were on offer inside. The modern fashion for new pub signs to replace originals when a pub is refurbished is disappointing to say the least – often a colourful and graphic sign with historical importance is replaced with an anodyne and characterless sign that looks just the same as the one hanging on the refurbished pub in the next village.

Nidderdale & Wharfedale

KEY

1 The Crown
2 Crown Hotel
3 Devonshire Arms
4 The Castle Inn
5 Early Doors
6 The Cock & Bottle
7 Royal Shepherd Inn
8 The Wooly Sheep Inn
9 Red Lion
10 The Albion
11 The Narrow Boat
12 The Craven Heifer
13 The Masons Arms
14 The Old Swan
15 Angel Inn
16 Devonshire Arms
17 The Fountaine Inn
18 The Old Hall Inn
19 The Gamekeeper's Inn
20 The Foresters Arms
21 The Devonshire
22 The Black Horse Hotel
23 Clarendon Hotel
24 Red Lion
25 The Devonshire Fell
26 Craven Arms
27 The New Inn
28 Tennant's Arms
29 The Falcon
30 Queens Arms
31 The Blue Bell Inn
32 The Racehorses
33 The King's Head
34 Thwaite Arms
35 Fox and Hounds
36 The Buck
37 The George Inn
38 The White Lion

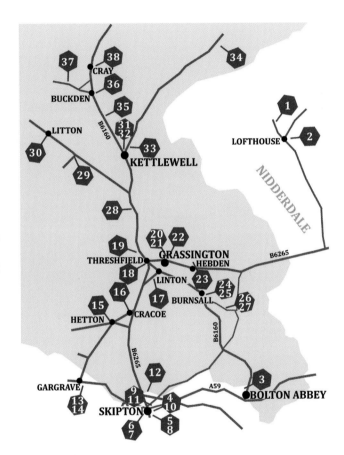

15

Malhamdale, Airedale and the Three Peaks Area

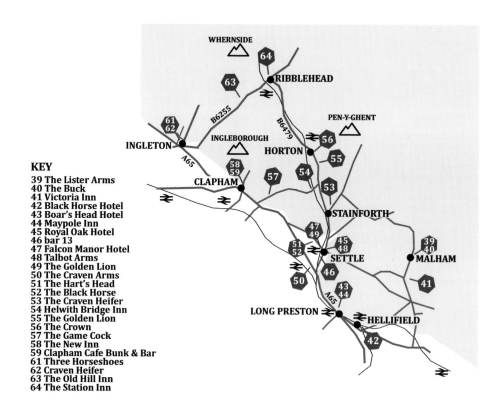

KEY

39 The Lister Arms
40 The Buck
41 Victoria Inn
42 Black Horse Hotel
43 Boar's Head Hotel
44 Maypole Inn
45 Royal Oak Hotel
46 bar 13
47 Falcon Manor Hotel
48 Talbot Arms
49 The Golden Lion
50 The Craven Arms
51 The Hart's Head
52 The Black Horse
53 The Craven Heifer
54 Helwith Bridge Inn
55 The Golden Lion
56 The Crown
57 The Game Cock
58 The New Inn
59 Clapham Cafe Bunk & Bar
61 Three Horseshoes
62 Craven Heifer
63 The Old Hill Inn
64 The Station Inn

Sedbergh, Dent, the Lune Valley and Westmoreland Dales

KEY

65 The Red Dragon
66 Sun Hotel
67 The Snooty Fox
68 Kings Arms Hotel
69 Royal Barn
70 The Pheasant Inn
71 The Barbon Inn
72 Swan Inn
73 The Dalesman
74 The Red Lion
75 George & Dragon
76 Sun Inn
77 The Sportsman's Inn
78 The Moorcock Inn
79 Black Swan
80 King's Head
81 The Fat Lamb
82 Black Bull
83 The Kings Arms Hotel
84 Pennine Hotel
85 White Lion
86 Black Bull
87 Bay Horse Inn

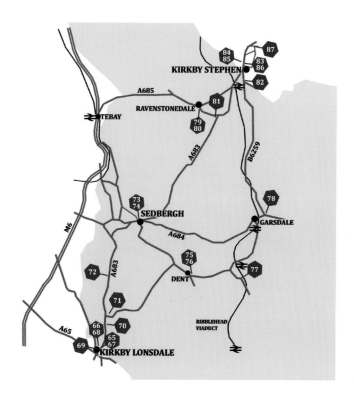

Swaledale, Arkengarthdale and Wensleydale

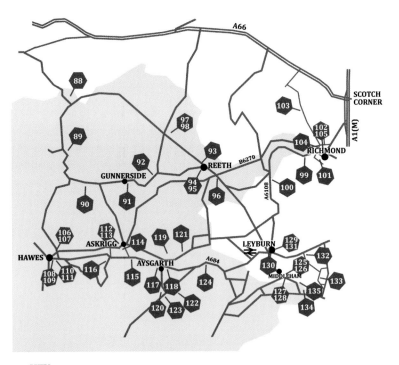

KEY

88 Tan Hill Inn
89 Keld Lodge
90 Farmer's Arms
91 King's Head
92 Punch Bowl Inn
93 The Buck
94 The Black Bull
95 King's Arms
96 The Bridge Inn
97 Red Lion
98 Charles Bathurst Inn
99 George & Dragon

100 The Bolton Arms
101 The Good Intent Inn
102 King's Head
103 Shoulder of Mutton
104 Unicorn Inn
105 Bishop Blaize Hotel
106 The Green Dragon
107 Simonstone Hall Hotel
108 The Crown
109 The Board Inn
110 The Fountain
111 White Hart Country In

112 The Crown Inn
113 The Kings Arms
114 The White Rose
115 Victoria Arms Inn
116 The Rose & Crown Hotel
117 George and Dragon Inn
118 Aysgarth Falls Hotel
119 The Wheatsheaf
120 The George Inn
121 Bolton Arms Inn
122 Fox & Hounds
123 Street Head Inn

124 The Wensleydale Heifer
125 The White Swan Hotel
126 The Black Bull
127 Dante
128 Richard III Hotel
129 Sandpiper Inn
130 Leyburn Bolton Arms
131 The Golden Lion
132 The Pheasant Inn
133 Old Horn Inn
134 The Blue Lion
135 The Cover Bridge Inn

NIDDERDALE

Upper Nidderdale

Nidd is a Celtic river name thought to mean 'brilliant'.

1. Crown Hotel, Middlesmoor

Main Street, Middlesmoor, Harrogate HG3 5ST
01423) 755204
crownmiddlesmoor@gmail.com
www.crownhotelmiddlesmoor.co.uk

This is the last pub in Nidderdale where the tarmaced road ends and becomes the Niddersdale Way footpath. It is a very traditional old pub that can boast some photos of the now demolished village built at nearby Scar House dam to house the construction workers and their families. The village name is first recorded in the 12th century and means 'moorland in the middle of two streams', referring to the River Nidd and its tributary, How Stean Beck. Alternatively, the name may come from a personal name, Midele, as seen in Middlesbrough.

2. Crown Hotel, Lofthouse

Thorpe Lane, Lofthouse, Harrogate HG3 5RZ
01423 755206

A handsome stone building at the western end of beautiful Nidderdale. An unusual panelled entrance corridor leads to a traditionally furnished, comfortable bar.

(What?ub, 28 March 2018)

WHARFEDALE

Wharfedale in snow, 2018

The valley of the winding river Wharfe – the winding river. In the 12th century it was Hwerverdale.

The Blue Bell, Kettlewell; The Fox & Hounds, Starbotton; The Falcon, Arncliffe; The George Inn, Hubberholme.

3. Devonshire Arms, Bolton Abbey

The Devonshire Arms Hotel & Spa, Bolton Abbey, Skipton North Yorkshire BD23 6AJ
01756 718100
res@devonshirehotels.co.uk
http://thedevonshirearms.co.uk/

Part of Devonshire Hotels & Restaurants – a collection of unique places owned by the Duke and Duchess of Devonshire, located in glorious locations on both the Bolton Abbey Estate and the Chatsworth Estate in Derbyshire. Not really a pub, the Devonshire Arms has a long tradition of hospitality: today's hotel was built in the early 17th century on the site of an inn. Today, the hotel has a number of fine bars.

The 4th Duke of Devonshire took it on in 1753 as part of the Bolton Abbey Estate. It was further developed by the 5th Duke, a man with considerable vision who exploited the tourist potential when he established miles of footpaths so that visitors could enjoy the splendid local views. The area was a magnet for poets and artists alike, including Wordsworth and Turner.

During the 19th century the royal family often stayed at Bolton Abbey for grouse shoots and The Devonshire Arms, which was often used for hospitality, expanded, so that by 1840 it could stable twenty horses and four carriages.

4. The Castle Inn, Skipton

2 Mill Bridge, Skipton BD23 1NJ
01756 796304
calvin.castleinn@gmail.com
www.thecastleinnskipton.co.uk

One of the unsung heroes of Yorkshire's celebrated confectionery industry heritage (Terry's, Rowntree's, Mackintosh, Needler's and others) – indeed of Skipton – is Claire Whitaker. It all began as a grocery and drapery shop in Crosshills run by John and Rebecca Whitaker around 1889. Their daughter Ida, a trained baker, persuaded her father to specialise as a baker's and confectioner's. He did, and produce was made in a room behind the shop, sold in the front while the family lived above. They moved in 1926 to the High Street, Skipton, and opened a restaurant above the shop. Claire, after whom the shop is today named, was the mother of John Whitaker, who is still chairman of the firm today and grandmother of William, the current managing director. Among their bestsellers are Mint Wafer, Mint Cremes and Mint Crisp made with an old family recipe; these are currently the world's bestselling after-dinner mint chocolates and are to be found in hotels (usually on your pillow), in restaurants, on aircraft and in supermarkets as own brands as well as in the usual sweet shops. In 1999 Chocolate Neapolitan was successfully launched: half a million of these are made every day out of an average daily production total of 1,500,000 chocolates.

5. Early Doors, Skipton

14 Newmarket Street, Skipton BD23 2HX
07517 334142
www.earlydoorspub.co.uk

This is a micro-pub named after the sitcom about a Manchester pub and nothing to do with its opening hours. No frills, no music, no WiFi and no food – just good beer and chat.

6. The Cock & Bottle, Skipton

30 Swadford Street, Skipton BD23 1RD
01756 794734
thecockandbottleskipton@gmail.com
www.cockandbottleskipton.co.uk

This is a former 18th century coaching inn with a single long, split-level bar and stone fireplaces. Mind the low beam above the step halfway along the bar. 'Cock & Bottle' was a common name for public houses and refers to the availability of liquor in draught or bottled form, the 'cock' being the name for the tap in the front of a barrel. The actual date of the building is unknown, although there has been a building on the site from the late 17th century.

Prostitutes reputedly entertained the navvies working on the Leeds–Liverpool Canal in the small rooms up in the gables at the front of the building. The exterior wall in the back yard bears a plaque denoting 'K.S. 1729' – after Katherine Sugden, the owner then.

7. Royal Shepherd Inn, Skipton

Canal Street, Skipton BD23 1LB
01756 797507

This is probably the only Royal Shepherd in the country. It is a canal-side, town-centre local; the main bar has an interesting canal-themed stained-glass.

8. The Wooly Sheep Inn, Skipton

38 Sheep Street, Skipton BD23 1HY
01756 700966 www.woollysheepinn.co.uk info@woollysheepinn.co.uk

9. Red Lion, Skipton

27 High Street, Skipton BD23 1DX
01756 790718
7926@greeneking.co.uk
www.redlion-skipton.co.uk

This is probably Skipton's oldest pub built as it was in 1205; it also claims to be Skipton's most haunted.

10. The Albion, Skipton

27 Otley Street, Skipton BD23 1EL
01756 794793

Parts of this pub date back to the 16th century.

11. The Narrow Boat, Skipton

36–38 Victoria Street, Skipton BD23 1JE
01756 797922
www.markettowntaverns.co.uk/pub-and-bar-finder/yorkshire/the-narrow-boat/
narrowboat@markettowntaverns.co.uk

12. The Craven Heifer, Skipton

Grassington Road, Skipton BD23 3LA
01756 792521
info@cravenheiferskipton.co.uk
www.cravenheiferskipton.co.uk

This craven heifer (1807–1812) was bred by the Rev. W. Carr in 1807 on the Duke of Devonshire's estate weighing in at 312 stone 8 lb and measuring from the tip of her nose to her rump 11 feet 4 inches. A wonderful animal. She was bought by Mr John Watkinson of Halton East for £200 and taken to Smithfield by a Mr G. Pickop and a Mr J. Kitchen. The journey to London took 73 days from the 19 November to 30 January 1812, during which time she was proudly shown at towns and cities on the way. Sadly, the craven heifer met an ignominious end when she was won in a cockfight.

The Lost Pubs Project gives these lost pubs of Skipton with year of closure where known:

Commercial, 38 Water Street.
Craven Arms, 12 Newmarket Street.
Hole in The Wall, High Street.
Lock Stock & Barrel, Coach Street.
Railway, 10 Carleton Street.
Royal Oak, 2 Water Street.
Ship, 1970s Gargrave Road. Why, when it is miles from the sea ? Because it was close to the Leeds–Liverpool Canal.
Snaygill Arms, Keighley Road.
Unicorn Hotel, Keighley Road.
http://www.closedpubs.co.uk/
yorkshire/skipton.html

A fine day out from The Hole in the Wall.

13. The Masons Arms, Gargrave

Marton Road, Gargrave, Nr Skipton, North Yorkshire BD23 3NL
01756 749304
info@masonsarmsgargrave.co.uk
http://www.masonsarmsgargrave.co.uk/index.htm

I wish I could say that this was the Woolly Sheep Inn in Sheep Street but it's not; it's The Railway.

There is a crown-green bowling green behind the pub.

Gargrave means Gara's grove or the copse in a triangular plot of land (Old Norse + Old English). Gargrave had its very own witch: Anne Greene, described in this extract from *Witchcraft in Yorkshire* by Patricia Crowther:

> *Anne Greene of Gargrave was examined by John Asheton and Roger Coats in 1853. John Tatterson testified, and this is how the clerk of the court reported it. Being disabled in body he, was troubled with ill spirits. He asked Anne's advice for pain in the ear. She told him that black wool was good for it, whereupon she crossed his left ear three times with her garter and got some hair out of his neck without his consent. When he got home he suffered more pain than before, and returned to her and said 'to look to it or he would look to her'. Having crossed his ear three times again, she said it would mend, and, with corruptible matter running out, it did. The accused herself explained that she, knowing a charm for curing earache, twice used it on Tatterson by crossing her garter over his ear and saying 'Boate help' (this was the name of an old god). For a pain in the head she required the patient's water and a lock of hair, which she boiled together, and threw into the fire. The verdict of the jury of life and death was not guilty.*

In the 1820s the main industry in Gargrave was cotton manufacturing with many warehouses alongside of the canal. The population at this time was 972 and there were several public houses including the Masons Arms and the Swan Inn. The Old Swan is Grade II listed.

The Pennine Way and the Leeds–Liverpool Canal pass through the village.

The Leeds–Liverpool Canal links the cities of Leeds and Liverpool via Bradford. It is 127 miles long, crosses the Pennines and includes 91 locks on the main line. It was first used in 1784 and results from the burgeoning mid-18 century industrial towns of Yorkshire including Leeds, Wakefield and Bradford. While the Aire & Calder Navigation served the east for Leeds, links to the west were limited. Bradford merchants wanted to increase the supply of limestone to make lime for mortar and agriculture using coal from Bradford's collieries and to transport textiles to Liverpool.

14. The Old Swan, Gargrave

20 High Street, Gargrave, Skipton BD23 3RB
01756 749232
info@old-swan-inn.co.uk
http://old-swan-inn.co.uk/

This is a three-storey former coaching inn. There was another pub here called the Grouse, in the High Street.

15. Angel Inn, Hetton

Hetton, Near Skipton, North Yorkshire BD23 6LT
01756 730263
info@angelhetton.co.uk
http://www.angelhetton.co.uk/

An 15th century drovers' inn, the Angel has forever been at the heart of the locality and is one of the UK's first true gastro pubs.

Hetton derives from the farm on the heathland (Old English) or the village on the hill. The origin of the name of the pub is not quite as obvious as it may seem. It probably has nothing to do with celestial angels but has its origins in the Angelot, a French coin minted from 1340 and popularised in England by Edward IV from 1465 when it was regarded as an efficacious touch-piece in the ubiquitous ceremony of touching by monarchs to cure the King's Evil, probably TB.

Hetton does not have a monopoly on this: many Angel pubs are thus named, including the famous Angel Islington.

For this and more fascinating local history, paintings, walks and local recipes, see Ian Scott Massie's *The Dale of Angels*, available only from The Angel.

The Angel around 1850

16. Devonshire Arms, Cracoe

Grassington Road, Cracoe BD23 6LA
01756 730237
info@thedevonshirearmsinn.com
www.devonshirearmsinn.co.uk

This is a coaching inn dating back to the sixteenth century. Crow hill (Old Norse). The nearby Cracoe Reef Knolls are geological remnants of an ancient coral reef. Cracoe was the home of the original 'Calendar Girls'.

17. The Fountaine Inn, Linton in Craven

The Fountaine Inn, Linton in Craven, North Yorkshire BD23 5HJ
01756 752210
info@fountaineinnatlinton.co.uk
http://www.fountaineinnatlinton.co.uk/

Linton means the farm where flax is grown (Old English), near Grassington. Lipton in the Domesday Book then Lynton in 1150. The village has many delightful features including the Falls, a fourteenth century packhorse bridge, 'Little Emily's Bridge'; almshouses by Vanbrugh (?) and the famous ancient stepping-stones, below an old (renovated) mill house.

Linton was a parish in Staincliffe Wapentake in the West Riding of Yorkshire. The ancient parish included the townships of Grassington, Hebden and Threshfield, all of which became separate civil parishes in 1866. Linton was transferred to North Yorkshire in 1974.

This historic whitewashed inn stands in a fascinating backwater, overlooking a tiny green but with Vanbrugh's typically monumental Fountaine hospital and almshouses to one side. The pub is one of five in the Skipton-based Individual Inns group.

(Martin Wainwright, *The Guardian,* 3 May 2012)

Ian Goldthorpe explains where the pub's name comes from:

Richard Fountaine of Linton made his fortune in London. By his will of July 15, 1721 an estate was purchased to provide revenue and the chapel and almshouses known as Fountaine's Hospital were erected on his main estate in Linton. £26 per year was to be spent on 6 poor men or women in the parish and £20 per year to the minister [if he resided in the parish, for reading prayers twice every week]. The Palladian style building may have been designed by William Wakefield, following the style of Vanburgh. The hospital was extended to the rear in the late 19th century. This followed a period of decay of the buildings and corruption among those in charge of the foundation. The hospital still houses local elderly people and the large estate purchased by Richard Fountaine continues to fund the charity.

(I. Goldthorpe (1998) *Grassington Towards the Millennium*. Grassington: The Dales Book Centre)

The pub has a tradition for games of 'ringing the bull'.

Barden Triangle includes mystical places with supernatural characteristics such as Troller's Gill, the conical knoll of Elbolton Hill (the 'Hill of the Fairies') and the Dibble's Bridge allegedly built by the Devil. Villages lying within the triangle include Appletreewick, Burnsall, Linton and Grassington.

Linton Falls was first built in 1909 but abandoned in 1948. In 2012 it was restored when a hydroelectric plant was constructed to provide electricity.

18. The Old Hall Inn, Threshfield

Old Hall Inn, Threshfield, Skipton BD23 5HB
01756 752441
www.oldhallinnandcottages.co.uk

The Angles founded Threshfield. Threshfield means open land where threshing takes place (Old English thresc). Freschefelt in Domesday.

Before 1066 the Domesday Book tells us that the Viking Gamel Bern was the landowner of here and Grassington, farming 840 acres of ploughland. After 1066 it became part of the lands of Gilbert Tison. By 1118 Tison was discredited and his lands returned to the king and then given to the honours of Percy, Ramilly, Fitz John and d'Aubigny. Gamel Bern was the bairn of Gamel, Thegn of Mercia, and he the son of Orm or Ulf. This family held the most land in Northern England.

The Old Hall is a Georgian inn that takes its name from the 14th century hall at the back; it was built by monks and reputedly the oldest inhabited building in Wharfedale. In the 16th century, Threshfield was part of a huge deer park.

Threshfield is home to Wharfedale Rugby Union Football Club who currently compete in the the third tier National League One. Their Avenue stadium holds 2,000 spectators, and was described as a 'sporting nirvana' by broadcaster John Inverdale. 'If there is a more wonderful sporting venue in the country for serious sport, I've yet to visit it', he wrote in the *Daily Telegraph*.

19. The Gamekeeper's Inn, Threshfield

Long Ashes Park, Threshfield, North Yorkshire BD23 5PN
01756 752434
events@gamekeeperinn.co.uk
http://www.gamekeeperinn.co.uk/

As you might expect from the name, this was once a gamekeeper's cottage for nearby Netherside Hall. The gamekeeper would have worked in the deer park hereabouts.

20. The Foresters Arms, Grassington

20 Main Street, Grassington, Skipton, North Yorkshire BD23 5AA
01756 752349
info@forestersarmsgrassington.co.uk
http://www.forestersarmsgrassington.co.uk/

Coaching inn origins. Coarse and fly-fishing permits for Saltaire Angling Club stretch on River Wharfe can be bought at the pub. Branch Community Pub of the Year 2017.

Logically, the name Grassington means grazing land farm. Or it could be town of Gersent or Gersendis.

Yarnbury Henge is nearby, a more or less circular neolithic monument. The picture shows an inclined mine entrance near there, evidence of the lead mining that was prevalent in the area.

21. The Devonshire, Grassington

25–27 Main Street, Grassington, Skipton BD23 5AD
01756 752525
thedevonshiregrassington.co.uk

A stone-built hotel off the cobbled square, dating largely from the 18th century.

Mossdale Caverns: the boggy valley (Old Norse), and the site of Britain's worse potholing disaster when six potholers died in the extremely challenging cave system in 1967. The bodies were left *in situ*. The coroner

had the cave sealed and concrete was poured down the entrance. In 1971 this was re-opened, with the agreement of the bereaved families, and the bodies were reburied by their colleagues in 'Mud Caverns', a chamber at the far end of the system. The caverns are north of Grassington.

22. The Black Horse Hotel, Grassington

4 Garrs Lane, Grassington, North Yorkshire BD23 5AT
01756 752770
blackhorsegrassington@live.co.uk
http://www.blackhorsehotelgrassington.co.uk/

The Black Horse Hotel is an old 17th century coaching inn. Enjoy the 'quirkiness' of the undulating corridors. It was known as the King William IV until the end of the 18th century and later as the Prince Albert. A room at the rear of the hotel housed the Upper Wharfedale Museum until it moved to new premises in the square in 1979.

Rylestone, near Grassington, means farmstead by the stream (Old English rynel + tun). Rilestune in the Domesday Book. Near Grassington. Rylstone and District Women's Institute was the inspiration for the 2003 film *Calendar Girls*, although local scenes for the film were shot at nearby Kettlewell. Rylstone is the subject of Wordsworth's *The White Doe of Rylstone*.

23. Clarendon Hotel, Hebden

Hebden, Skipton BD23 5DE
01756 752446
www. clarendonhebden.co.uk

This pub dates back to the 18th century. House beer is Clarendon pale ale brewed by Wensleydale Brewery. There is a lounge bar and a separate dining room. One end of the main bar area is separated off as a snug, with a wood-burning stove, and is usually kept free for non-diners.

The name Hebden may be derived from either heope, Old English for a rose-hip or heopa, Old English for a bramble, and dene, Old English for a valley, or from the Scandinavian Hebban, a ridge forming an elevated site above a small valley. The Domesday Book refers to it as Hebedene held by Osbern d'Arques, of Thorpe Arch. In 1066 the land was held by Dreng, a Viking.

Perhaps the most famous Clarendon was Edward Hyde, 1st Earl of Clarendon (1609 –1674), Lord Chancellor to Charles II from 1658, two years before the Restoration of the Monarchy, until 1667. He was also one of England's most important historians, and was author of the most influential contemporary history of the Civil War, *The History of the Rebellion* (1702). He was the maternal grandfather of Queen Mary II and Queen Anne.

24. Red Lion, Burnsall

Burnsall, near Skipton, N. Yorkshire BD23 6BU
01756 720204
info@redlion.co.ukhttp://www.redlion.co.uk/
http://www.redlion.co.uk/

Looking out of the Red Lion into Burnsall

The cellars here date from the 12th century, and the original 'one up, one down' structure that is now the bar originates from the 16th century when it was a ferryman's inn. The Red Lion is on the Dalesway long-distance footpath and the Way of the Roses cycle route.

The 1086 *Doomsday Book* – the 'Great Survey' – tells us that 'in Brineshale, Dringlet had two carucates and two oxgangs to be taxed'; it was all devastated during William's 'Harrying of the North', his scorched earth policy for subduing the rebellious northerners after the Norman conquest by the Normans. A carucate is the amount of land cultivated by one plough in one year and a day (120 acres); an oxgang was the amount of land tillable by one ox in a ploughing season.

It all goes quiet then but we have numerous relics from the time when Robert de Romille took possession of Skipton, some of which can be seen in the church of St

Wilfrid. The oldest part of St Wilfrid dates from the 12th century with later elements from the 14th. The base of the font shows Norman ornamentation that would not be later than 1150. The list of records dates from the 13th century and a stone tablet records that this church was repaired and 'butified' by Sir William Craven who was Lord Mayor of London and on whom the tale of 'Dick Whittington' was based.

Burnsall, formerly Brinshall or Brineshale derives from either 'the hall by the burn' or, more likely, the hall of a chieftain named Burn, meaning ruler. The sufffix 'sal' in Danish means the main room or hall in Danish.

Burn was founder of a noble house – the Earls of Craven – giving his name to the local Craven district. He was born in Appletreewick of poor stock, moved to London, and took a job in a silk mercer's business. His rise to wealth and fame was swift – by 1611 he was Lord Mayor of London. He founded the old Grammar School adjoining the church which is now the local primary school.

25. The Devonshire Fell, Burnsall

Burnsall, Skipton BD23 6BT
01756 729000
www. devonshirefell.co.uk

Another property belonging to the Devonshires' Chatsworth Estate since 1998. 'The open-plan, comfortable bar area is bright and airy and is divided into several distinct areas.'

26. Craven Arms, Appletreewick

Appletreewick, Skipton BD23 6DA
01756 720270
info@craven-cruckbarn.co.uk
http://www.craven-cruckbarn.co.uk/index.html

Appletreewick, pronounced 'Aptrick', literally means the farm where apple trees grew. Wick, farm, may be Anglo-Saxon or Viking. The Tudor-style High Hall was restored by Sir William Craven, Appletreewick's own Dick Whittington, who became Sheriff and Lord Mayor of London in the early 17th century. He was born in what is now Appletreewick Church. 'Craven' is now a district of North Yorkshire. The pub sign is of the Craven Coat of Arms. Having made his fortune, Craven returned to Appletreewick to build Burnsall School and Burnsall Bridge.

Apparently, in 2009, an AA study of rural driving awarded Appletreewick the title of 'Britain's Friendliest Town to Drive Through' – based on data monitoring road rage, driver communication, average speeds and hand-wave acknowledgments of courteous driving. A punning sign at the approach to the village reads 'The Craven Arms – Gateway to the Ales'.

The Craven Arms began life as a farm house in the 16th century, evolving into the pub we see today. Beer started flowing when the resident farming family sold ale from the kitchen window as a means of supplementing income. Rooms were added and a horse and coach stop

with food. More recent additions are the Cruck Barn and Shepherd huts at the rear, available for functions of all kinds, including ferret racing.

The 'Inspirational Toilets' have to be seen; they are men's and women's toilets, decorated with pictures of heroes, pioneers and inspiring figures from today and yesteryear. Don't ask; there was no one in the Ladies' at the time. See also the Dambusters and metal detector displays with findings from the area.

The dining room used to be the stables for the coach stop. When it was a farm the original use was to house livestock and store animal feed. The cattle sheltered in the 'Mo' or ground floor; their feed would be stored up on the 'baulks' or balcony. The seven metre high roof of oak truss work, sheep's wool insulation and a heather thatch, were all sourced locally. The walls are from stone found on site pointed with lime mortar and plastered using a traditional lime, river sand and horse hair mix. It was all finished off with a lime wash as used in barns and stables in the past.

Heather thatched roofs were once a common sight in the area before stone slates; the steep pitch of the roof assists in the weather proofing of the heather. A very rare sight nowadays.

27. The New Inn, Appletreewick

The New Inn, Main Street, Appletreewick, North Yorkshire BD23 6DA
01756 720 252
newinnapptree@gmail.com
https://www.thenewinnappletreewick.co.uk

The New Inn was called 'The New Inn' because, having been built in the 1850s/1860s, it was not as old as the rest of the village. One landlord, an eccentric Mr Showers, felt that the Wharfe Valley bore 'many landmarks reminiscent of the Viking invasion' so he thought 'Why not bring Denmark back to the Dales?' Showers introduced Smørrebrød and five beers brewed by Tuborg Breweries of Copenhagen. The New Inn was thus the first in the UK to offer Tuborg. Smørrebrød consists of a piece of buttered rye bread (rugbrød), and pålæg – the topping, that can be cold cuts, pieces of meat or fish, cheese or spreads. This is essentially the famous Danish open sandwich.

Showers was one of the first landlords to introduce a smoking ban in his pub. The death of a close friend from lung cancer led Showers to clear the bar of every last cigarette, cigar and ashtray and introduce a ban on smoking for all time.

Nearby Troller's Gill is the troll's arse ravine. Old Norse + Old English + Old Norse: troll + ears + gill. The 'Yorkshire Dales' website describes it best:

> Troller's Gill is a sinister little ravine at the head of Trollerdale near …
> Appletreewick … Legend has it that this narrow limestone gorge is the
> haunt of the 'Barquest' or 'Barguest' – the terrifying spectral hound of
> Craven (which is said to have 'eyes as big as saucers', and which may have
> even given part of the inspiration for Sir Arthur Conan Doyle's Sherlock
> Holmes story 'The Hound of the Baskervilles'). The nooks, caves and
> crannies of Troller's Gill are also said to be the home of Scandinavian trolls,
> evil bloodsucking gnomes, flesh-eating boggarts, hideous gargoyle-like
> rock sprites, deranged goblins, predatory pixies and maliciously twisted
> imps – and perhaps even other sorts of similarly diabolical and fiendishly
> unpleasant beings lying in wait for the unsuspecting rambler … The trolls
> in particular are said to hurl rocks down on passers-by walking through
> the ravine … Near the head of the gill there are a series of disued mine
> workings as well as natural caves and potholes – including the ominously
> named 'Hell Hole': Troller's Gill is not a place to be visited alone.

(http://www.yorkshire-dales.com/trollers-gill.html, accessed 24 October 2015)

The barquest can turn you to stone with just one look.

28. Tennant's Arms, Kilnsey

Kilnsey, Skipton, North Yorkshire BD23 5SP
01756 753946
chrishyde1@outlook.com
https://www.thetennantsarms.co.uk/

The Tennant's Arms was once an important 17th century coaching stop on the route from Richmond to London. The pub is named after the Tennant family that owned the Kilnsey Estate up to 1911; what is now the Kilnsey trout farm is next door.

Kilnsey means the marsh by the kiln in Old English – cyln + saege – a reference to the lime burning here. Domesday calls it Chileseie. Kilnsey is famous for Kilnsey Crag, which is around 170 feet high, with an overhang of 40 feet. Kilnsey Crag was painted by Turner in 1816. West from Kilnsey towards Malham Tarn runs the historic Mastiles Lane, a Roman marching road, later an important route for sheep from the Fountains Abbey to summer pasture on higher ground. The Old Hall was a medieval administrative site for the local wool trade. Most of the present building dates from 1658.

29. The Falcon, Arncliffe

2 Castle Yd, Arncliffe, Skipton BD23 5QE
01756 770205
thefalconinnatarncliffe@yahoo.com
www.thefalconinn.com

A true gem of a pub. Many pubs in the Dales vaunt their antiquity and many indeed are old and unspoilt. The Falcon, however, is the last word in the tradition of authentic English pubs.

Arncliffe means cliff of the eagles from the Old English earn, eagle, sadly no more in this attractive Littondale village on the River Skirfare. The pub here, the Falcon, is ancient and typical of early public houses, which were essentially a private house in which the beer was brewed in an adjoining beer house out the back and dispensed in a room from cask into a jug and then into your glass. This is still the way it is

served to this day. Arncliffe was the setting for the fictional village of Beckindale in the ITV soap opera *Emmerdale Farm*, from 1972 until it moved to Esholt. The Falcon was The Woolpack.

Among other fascinating stuff in this real pub is a fading photo of a champion marrow from 1900, armchairs and settees, and Timothy Taylor ale served in ceramic jugs from wooden barrels.

Two of those modern hand-pumps serve you too: they'll never catch on ...

What?ub says:

> Unspoilt, traditional, ivy clad Dales pub-cum-hotel on the village green. Mullioned bay windows front a pub that eschews modern gimmickry and the last significant changes to its pub interior all happened in the 1950s. It was at that time that the small servery was introduced where the beer was served direct from the cask by jug ... Note: you can still have the beer served from the jug!

The Arncliffe to Malham Road

30. Queens Arms, Litton

The Queens Arms, Litton, Skipton, North Yorkshire BD23 5QJ
01756 770096
info@queensarmslitton.co.uk
http://queensarmslitton.co.uk/

The Queens Arms is a traditional 17th century inn. Built in 1630, it became a pub in 1843 and still boasts open fires, mullioned windows, oak beamed ceilings and a stone-flagged bar area. The Queens was home to the Litton Brewery but brewing is currently in abeyance; the brewing equipment is still on-site.

The original pub here was down a lane between the road and the river; it is now used as a barn. Mrs Taylor, one of the landladies, cleverly evaded paying for her

licence by selling 1d or 1/d parkin – and beer to wash it down.

Litton maybe means the farm on the hill slope (Old Norse + Old English hlith); Domesday: Litone. Alternatively, it means a village on a roaring stream. Littondale is the valley with the farm on a hill slope (Old Norse + Old Norse/Old English). Notable for not being named after its river, the Skirfare. Once Littunedale in the 12th century.

The hamlet of Cosh was the last house in the dale, which before 2011 was 'the most remote home in the Dales with no electricity, no gas, no mains water and accessible only by off-road vehicles up a rough mile-and-half-long track'. In the 1950s the inhabitants of Cosh were offered electricity but declined as they didn't want to pay the bills. Cosh means the hut in the green open pastures (Middle English + Old English).

31. The Blue Bell Inn, Kettlewell

Middle Lane, Kettlewell, North Yorks BD23 5QX
01756 760230
bluebell@hotelchannelmanager.co.uk
https://www.bluebellkettlewell.co.uk

Established in 1860, this former coaching inn is the oldest pub in the village. Kettlewell is Anglo-Saxon and derives from Chetelewelle – a bubbling spring or stream; Old English cetel + wella. In the 13th century the Thursday market mostly sold corn outside the King's Arms. Later, textiles and lead mining were important to the local economy. The remains of the smelting-mill, which flourished from 1700 to 1880, can still be seen near the confluence of Cam Gill and Dowber Gill Becks half a mile above the village.

Kettlewell was the village of Knapely in the 2003 film *Calendar Girls*.

32. The Racehorses, Kettlewell

The Green, Kettlewell, Skipton, North Yorkshire BD23 5RD
01756 761600
http://www.thekingsheadkettlewell.co.uk/

A fine 18th century hotel on the River Wharfe at the Town Foot bridge in the centre of Kettlewell. Its name derives from a corruption of 'trace horses' – horses that were used to provide extra (horse) power for coaches on steep hills; Kettlewell is noted for its steep hill roads leading out of the village.

33. The King's Head, Kettlewell

The Green, Kettlewell, Skipton, North Yorkshire BD23 5RD
01756 761600
kingsheadkettlewell@outlook.com
www. thekingsheadkettlewell.co.uk

The bar area boasts stone flags and a huge fireplace with inglenook seating.

34. Thwaite Arms, Horsehouse in Coverdale

Thwaite Arms, Horsehouse in Coverdale DL8 4TS
01969 640206

The pub dates from 1808 in the dale of the River Cover, a tributary of the Ure. It extends south-west from the eastern end of Wensleydale to the dale head at Park Rash Pass, between Great Whernside to the south and Buckden Pike to the north. Coverdale cheese comes from the valley – a variant of Wensleydale cheese, produced at the Wensleydale Creamery in Hawes.

35. Fox and Hounds, Starbotton

Starbotton, Skipton, North Yorkshire BD23 5HY
01756760269
info@foxandhoundsstarbotton.co.uk
http://www.foxandhoundsstarbotton.co.uk/

The pub sign shows a wily fox outfoxing the hounds; a previous one was even better with the fox actually riding one of the horses.

Starbotton means the valley bottom where stakes are cut (Old Norse stafn + botn). The Domesday Book had it as Stamphotne. Alternatively, it may derive from 'Stauerboten' – 12th century – Old English 'stæfer' replacing the Norse 'stafn'.

The house with a pointed arch window next to the pub was built for the manager of the Smelt Mill. The barn with an external staircase, restored in 2009, on the bend in the road opposite the Fox and Hounds, once housed a drovers' bar on the upper floor. Beasts were accommodated at ground level. Heading towards Buckden, the last house on the right hand side is below road level. This was the original pub in the village. For many years there was a vast pile of rubble to the north of the former pub. This came from a large barn that, to quote one of the oldest residents in his 90s, 'collapsed when my wife looked at it'.

Just before the bridge there is a small gatehouse beside the entrance gateway to a Victorian house; the roof was smashed by a loose tank gun, which swung out of control, in a convoy moving through the Dale just before D-Day. The owner at the time was too patriotic to claim the costs of the repair and it was not refurbished until the early 2000s. Disaster struck the village in June 1686 when a flash flood caused much of the village to be swept away.

Starbotton boasts a Quaker burial ground. The Smelt Flue remains, leading up to the Smelt Chimney above Cam Gill – remnants of the Smeltmill. You can still crawl through parts of the flue – the old job for children at the mill was to collect white lead oxide from the sides of the flue, which explains the high number of young people buried in the churchyard at Kettlewell in the 18th and 19th centuries.

36. The Buck, Buckden

Skipton BD23 5JA
01756 761401
info@buckinnbuckden.co.uk
www.buckinnbuckden.co.uk

A wonderful pub in a wonderful setting. The best Dales news so far this year is that the Buck re-opened in June 2018 after a comprehensive and stylish refurbishment. Anyone who knows the old version will be amazed at just how capacious and airy this pub now is.

Buckden is a picturesque village in upper Wharfedale where the pub, The Buck, shares its name; apparently, there were two other pubs in the village at one time. The etymology derives from the Old English words bucca and denu meaning he-goat, or buck, and valley.

Buckden was founded by the Normans as the centre for the hunting forest of Langstrothdale Chase, one of ten hunting forests in the dales controlled until 1534 by the Percy family. It is on the Roman road from Ilkley (Olicana) to the fort at Bainbridge (Virosidum). Buckden Rake follows the path of this road, through Rakes Wood to Cray and over Stake Moss. Lead mining was developed above Buckden in 1697 at the Buckden Gavel mine on Buckden Pike. In 1964, a skeleton was found in Buckden Gavel mine: it was never identified and was nicknamed 'Buckden Bill'; coins and a funeral card found amongst the bones suggest that it dates from 1890. The bridge at Buckden is called the 'Election bridge' because, when the bridge at Hubberholme was destroyed by flooding in the late 18th century, the prospective local MP promised to give £200 towards the cost of a new bridge if he was elected.

Tragically, on 30 January 1942 a Wellington bomber with a Polish crew crashed on Buckden Pike in a snowstorm. Only rear gunner Joseph Fusniak survived; he followed the tracks of a fox down from the Pike to safety at the White Lion in Cray. In 1973, he built the memorial to his compatriots on the mountain. The late Denis Healey, Labour Chancellor of the Exchequer (1974–1979), spent his honeymoon in a converted stable next to the Buck Inn.

Buckden Pike height: 702 m (2,303 feet).

Buckden was described somewhat mystically (and mysteriously) by Alfred Wainwright in his *A Pennine Journey* as 'perched on a hillside like a Tibetan monastery'. Too much Old Peculier? In 1892 E. Bogg described how 'the dark green of the firs and the wild-looking glens present an appearance of weird grandeur truly Alpine'.

37. The George Inn, Hubberholme

Kirk Gill, Hubberholme, Skipton BD23 5JE
01756 760223
visit@thegeorge-inn.co.uk
http://www.thegeorge-inn.co.uk/

The George stands in a beautiful place overlooking the river Wharfe in the hamlet of Hubberholme, and is one of the few remaining un-modernised inns in the Dales. Formerly a farmstead, then a vicarage, the George dates from the 1600s. Remote and unspoilt, it is a Grade II listed, whitewashed building with mullioned windows, thick stone walls, heavy oak beams and flagged floors.

J. B. Priestley (1894 –1984) was a fan. His real love in life was for the Yorkshire Dales, of which he, a truly global traveller, wrote:

> *For variety of landscape these Dales cannot be matched on this island or anywhere else. A day's walk among them will give you almost everything fit to be seen on this earth.*

(From his Introduction to *The Beauty of Britain*, 1935)

> *These Yorkshire Dales are … the most rewarding countryside I have ever known. Is this simply local patriotism or the memory of early enchanted days ? It is not … You have come down from Wuthering Heights into Arcadia.*

(J.B Priestley, *Life International*, 1966)

Two years after his death in 1984 the ashes of Priestley were scattered in the St Michael and All Angels churchyard in Hubberholme. He described Hubberholme as 'one of the smallest, pleasantest places in the world' (*The Other Place*, 1953). The church is next to the George Inn – a favourite Priestley refuge. Elsewhere, he described Hubberholme as 'Hubberholme – just bridge, an inn and a church, all old – is sheer magic, not quite in this world' (*Life International,* 1966). The church dates mainly from the 12th century, the oak roof however was completed in 1558. The church's oak pews were crafted by Kilburn's Robert Thompson, whose trademark mouse can be spotted secreted in the woodwork. Note also the chapel's rood loft.

The bridleway over the Horse Head Pass to Yockenthwaite in Langstrothdale was routinely used by the priest from Hubberholme to reach his chapel in Halton Gill. To the west, paths lead to Pen-y-ghent via Plover Hill.

When the vicar was at home he would light a candle in the window as a beacon to his parishioners. This tradition survives today with a candle lit whenever the bar is open and serving. The candle is also used in the annual land-letting auction known as the Hubberholme Parliament and is held on the first Monday night of the year in a tradition dating back centuries. The local farmers gather to bid for 16 acres of pastureland owned by the church, the proceedings of which go to help the poor people of the parish. The vicar oversees the proceedings and sits in the House of Lords (dining room) while the bidding takes place in the House of Commons (the bar). The highest bid made when the candle flickers out wins the auction.

Scar House nearby is on the hill overlooking Hubberholme on the way to Cray. The current building is Victorian, however a previous house was visited by George Fox in 1652 while he was trying to convert Seekers to Quakers. At the time the house was owned by James Tennant who was later executed in York for religious reasons. The house was the first land owned by the Quakers and contains a Quaker burial ground, although there are no headstones to be seen.

Scaling crag at Kilnsey, next door to the Tennant's Arms [#28]

38. The White Lion, Cray

Cray, Skipton BD23 5JB
01756 760262
info@whitelioninncray.com

A former drovers' inn, the White Lion dates from the mid-1600s and is the highest pub in Wharfedale. It is next to Cray Gill beneath Buckden Pike. According to What?ub:

The main bar area is stone-flagged with three distinct areas on two levels and with a roaring fire. The bar-top is made from a single piece of oak and the side room has been furnished with settees and comfy chairs to create a snug, complete with wood-burning stove.

The recent refurbishment – while very smart and tasteful – has inevitably sanitised what was a superb, unspoilt muddy boots Dales pub.

'White Lions' are associated with the Yorkist Edward IV (r. 1461–70; 1471–1483).

MALHAMDALE AND AIREDALE

Malham Cove

39. The Lister Arms, Malham

Gordale Scar Road, Malham, Skipton BD23 4DB
01729830444
info@listerarms.co.uk
https://www.thwaites.co.uk/lister-arms-malham/

A large stone Grade II listed inn dating from 1723, overlooking the village green. It is named after Thomas Lister, owner of the Manor of Gisburn, twelve miles to the south. Thomas Lister, 4th Baron Ribblesdale (1854–1925), was a Liberal politician; he was born in Fontainebleau, France. He held the office of Lord-in-Waiting to HM Queen Victoria between 1880 and 1885 and was Master of the Royal Buckhounds between 1892 and 1895.

The pub is a traditional coaching inn: the mounting block can still be seen; there is a fine tiled entrance hall.

45

40. The Buck, Malham

**Cove Road, Malham Nr Skipton, North
Yorkshire BD23 4DA
01729 830317**

**info@thebuckmalham.co.uk
www.thebuckmalham.co.uk**

Rebuilt in 1820 on the site of an old coaching inn; there is a separate low-ceilinged, stone-flagged Hikers' Bar (with its own entrance) with a huge wood-burning stove. Malham Cove, Malham Tarn, Janet's Foss and Gordale Scar are all nearby.

The mosaic on the floor was gifted by John Ruskin.

Gordale Scar by James Ward (ca. 1812)

Janet's Foss

Foss is the Old Norse word for a waterfall or force while Janet (or Jennet) was the queen of the local fairies who live behind the falls in a cave, Janet's Cave; this was (with better historicity) inhabited by smelters working the copper mines at nearby Pikedaw to the west. The foss is used as a natural sheep dip by local farmers.

Gordale means the dirty valley or the valley covered with manure (Old Norse + Old Norse/Old English). It is a limestone ravine that contains two waterfalls and has overhanging limestone cliffs over 100 metres high. The gorge could have been formed by water from melting glaciers or by a cavern collapse.

Wordsworth wrote in the sonnet 'Gordale', 'let thy feet repair to Gordale chasm, terrific as the lair where the young lions couch'; Turner painted it in 1816: the result now hangs in Tate Britain.

In nearby Calton – which means the farm where calves are kept (Old English) – in 1851 seventy-five people lived here, of whom thirty-three went by the name of Shackleton, resident in five households.

Malham means the hollows: 'malr' means 'shaped like a sack'. which probably refers to the cove. Malhamdale is the valley near the coves (Old Norse). The ham part is not an Anglo-Saxon name, which is what you might expect. The Tarn is from ON tjorn (pool); the cove from Old English cofa. It was Malgum in the Domesday Book. The dale was Malghedale in 1199.

41. Victoria Inn, Kirkby Malham

Skipton BD23 4BS
01729 830499
www.victoriainnkirkbymalham.co.uk

Built in 1840, next to the impressive parish church. Kirkby Malham means the farmstead by the church near Malham (Old Norse); it was Kirkeby Malham in 1154. A free grammar school was founded here in 1606 by John Topham, for twenty to thirty children to receive an English education; Latin and Greek were taught free.

42. Black Horse Hotel, Hellifield

Main Road, Hellifield, Skipton BD23 4HT
01729 851402

131; 131 INSET

Renowned for its collection of musical instruments above the bar and elsewhere.

Hellifield means Helgi's or Halga's open land (Old Norse personal name + Old English; or holy field from Old English haelig + feld. The Domesday Book lists as Helgfeld, Helgeflet and Haelgefeld; the village may also have been dedicated to the Anglo-Saxon Goddess 'Hel' so that the name derives from the Norse 'The Farm of Helgi'. In the 12th century, Hellifield was 'Nether Hellifield' and in the 17th and 18th centuries 'Hellifield Pele' and later 'Hellifield Cochins'. In the Middle Ages, the area was plagued by grey wolves, so Hellifield men were employed to guide travellers in the vicinity to safety.

43. Boar's Head Hotel, Long Preston

Main Street, Long Preston, Skipton BD23 4ND
01729 840217
boarsheadhotel@hotmail.co.uk
www.boarsheadlongpreston.co.uk

A pleasant 1700s Dales country inn. The derivation of Long Preston is 'the priest's farmstead' (Old English prcost). 'Long' was added to distinguish this from all the other 'Prestons', a nod to its linear development. Prestune in the Domesday Book. A school was built in the village during the reign of Edward IV (1461–1483) as part of the Hammerton Chapel, closed in 1541 during the dissolution of the religious houses. In 1672 the Petty School was held, most likely either in the chapel or in a building near an old vicarage. A new school replaced the Petty School in 1819. In 1790, a cotton mill was built on the site of an old corn mill. The mill was demolished in 1881 due to flooding after which Fleets cotton mill was built – three storeys high and water powered.

44. Maypole Inn, Long Preston

Main Street, Long Preston, Skipton BD23 4PH
01729 841066

THE THREE PEAKS AREA

The Three Peaks are:

Pen-y-Ghent

Pen-y-ghent, is 2,273 feet high and shares its name with Pen-y-fan, Pen y Gadair, Pen y Gaer, Pen y Parc, Pen y Rhwbyn and many others, in Wales. Pen-y- ghent is an echo of the times when most of the country we now know now as England spoke a language similar to Welsh. Pen usually means hill and y is the definite article 'the', so its name means

Pen-y-Ghent from Horton

the *something* hill; the meaning of ghent remains unknown for sure. It may mean 'edge' or 'border', making it 'Hill on the border'; or, it could mean 'wind' or 'winds' – transliterating from the Welsh, gwynt ('wind') thus making it 'Head of the Winds'.

Ingleborough

The fort on the hill (Old English ingel and burh). Ingleborough is the second highest mountain in the Dales, at 2,372 feet (723 m). In 1346 it was referred to as Ingelburc. Excavations at the peak have revealed the remains of an old walled enclosure (the fort) along with foundations of Iron Age huts. As many as 120,000 people climb Ingleborough each year.

Whernside

The hillside where querns or millstones were found (Old English cweorn + side).

Whernside from the B6255

45. Royal Oak Hotel, Settle

Market Place, Settle BD24 9ED
01729 822561
info@royaloak-settle.co.uk
www. royaloak-settle.co.uk

What?ub describes it well (16 February 2018):

> *A large, open-plan eighteenth-century inn, it has an interior of national importance and is listed in CAMRA's Britain's Best Real Heritage Pubs: extensively re-modelled by Duttons of Blackburn in the mid-1930s to create an idealised Olde Englishe panelled interior for the new breed of motorised tourists, the pub features lavish plasterwork imitation timber. Although the layout was much altered in the mid-1960s, much of the panelling remains in the main bar area and the separate dining/function room, some of it highly decorated. Entry is via a revolving door which is also noteworthy.*

Pubs named Royal Oak, of course, indicated that the owner was a supporter of Charles II; he hid in one at Boscobel after the battle of Worcester in 1651 before restoring the monarchy in 1660.

46. bar 13, Settle

(Formerly Thirteen Cafe Bar)
13 Duke Street, Settle BD24 9DU
01729 824356
patrick@bar13settle.co.uk
www.bar13settle.co.uk

A muddy boots kind of a wine bar with a reputation for its real ales. Magicked in 2005 out of a small hardware store on the main street, it is the nearest pub to the railway station.

47. Falcon Manor Hotel, Settle

Skipton Road, Settle BD24 9BD
01729823814
www.falconmanor.co.uk

This grand Grade II listed hotel built in 1841 features a high-ceilinged public bar behind the imposing front door, a tall period window, classic bird and hunting scene prints, a very wide bar, a solid stone bar back and meat hooks in the ceiling, a magnificent stairwell, a huge chandelier and 'peacock' chairs. Falcon Manor was built in 1841 for the Reverend Swale with money provided by his

two grandmothers. They were anxious to bequeath a pile that was befitting his status in the local community. Falcon Manor was what he got, although it was originally named Ingfield Hall, after the field in which it was built; the change of name took place after 1921. The fussy grandmothers also donated £500 toward the cost of building the new Settle church on the basis that their reverential grandson could be the first incumbent.

48. Talbot Arms, Settle

High Street, Settle, North Yorkshire BD24 9EX
01729 823924
info@talbotsettle.co.uk
www.talbotsettle.co.uk

Standing only five minutes' walk from Settle Railway station – the start of the famous 'Settle to Carlisle Line' – which runs through some of the most breathtaking scenery in the country. The Settle–Carlisle Railway climbs to its highest point at Aisgill Summit – 1,168 feet.

There have been three rail crashes on this stretch of line. The first was the Hawes Junction crash, which occurred on Christmas Eve 1910, between Hawes Junction and Aisgill, when twelve people lost their lives, some of whom were trapped in the wreckage and were burned to death. This was also the scene of the Aisgill rail accident in 1913 when two trains collided and caught fire: fourteen people in the first train died at the scene and two passengers later died of their injuries. Thirty-eight passengers in the second train were seriously injured. In 1995 a class 156 Super-Sprinter was derailed near here by a landslide and was subsequently run into by a train travelling in the opposite direction. The conductor of the first train died in the collision.

Talbots (also, for example, at Wetherby, Middlesbrough and Malton) signify a now extinct breed of large hunting dogs. Middlesbrough FC was formed at the Middlesbrough Talbot. The Naked Man Inn in Settle dates from 1663; he is happily matched with The Naked Woman one mile up the road in Langliffe dating from 1660. The Naked Man is the oldest café in the country. There is also the annual Settle Storytelling Festival. The Gallery on the Green is the smallest art gallery in the world: drawings, paintings, photographs and installations works are all on display housed in a former BT telephone kiosk.

49. The Lion, Settle

Duke Street, Settle, North Yorkshire BD24 9DU
01729 822203
https://www.thwaites.co.uk/hotels-and-inns/inns/lion-at-settle/

A former 17th century coaching inn, the Lion at Settle was originally called the Golden Lion. The Lion's Den, accessed off the street via the old 'dwarf door' dated 1671, is comfortable with wooden flooring and dark wood-panelling.

Settle has 7th century Anglian origins, its name being the Angle word for settlement. The Domesday Book reveals that until 1066 Bo was the lord of Setel but after the Harrying of the North (1069–1071) the land was gifted to Roger de Poitou. In 1249 a market charter was granted to Henry de Percy, 7th feudal baron of Topcliffe by Henry III.

Daniel Defoe in his *A Tour Thro' the Whole Island of Great* Britain (1724–1727), wrote 'Settle is the capital of an isolated little kingdom of its own surrounded by barren hills'.

Victoria Cave nearby was discovered in 1837 on the day of Queen Victoria's accession. The cave is a geological SSSI and scheduled monument. Victoria Cave contained fossil remains, the earliest of which are 130,000 years old, and include mammoth, straight-tusked elephant, cave bear and hippopotamus, bos primigenius, rhinoceros leptorhinus and spotted hyenas.

50. The Craven Arms, Giggleswick

Brackenber Lane, Giggleswick, Settle BD24 0EA
01729 825627 / 0781 752 4597
info@craven-arms.co.uk
http://craven-arms.co.uk/

The Craven Arms Hotel was formerly the Old Station Inn. A Plague Stone is outside – a shallow trough that, in times of plague, was filled with vinegar to sterilise the coins that were left by quarantined Giggleswick townspeople as payment for food brought from surrounding farms. There is a similar plague stone outside the Burtonstone Inn in York.

The Yorkshire Three Peaks is near here; the route is 24 miles long, and includes 5,200 feet (1,585 m) of climbing.

Giggleswick appears as Ghigeleswic in the Domesday Book meaning 'Dwelling or (dairy) farm of a someone called Gikel or Gichel'. An Old English or Middle English personal name, probably a short form of the biblical name Judichael + wīc. The parish church is dedicated to St Alkelda, an obscure Anglo-Saxon saint associated with Middleham.

Giggleswick features in *Hancock's Half Hour*, in *The Train Journey* episode, broadcast on 23 October 1959. Russell Harty was an English teacher at the famous school here at the same time that Richard Whiteley attended as a pupil.

The village of Wham is nearby – its name means the marshy hollow, nook or valley from Old English hwamm or Old Norse hvammer. A 13th century reference gives Quane. Likewise Feizor, which translates as Fech's upland pastures, Old Irish/Old Norse personal name + Old Norse. Fech was a landowner from the area before 1066.

51. The Hart's Head, Giggleswick

Belle Hill, Giggleswick, Settle BD24 0BA
01729 822086
info@hartsheadinn.co.uk
http://www.hartsheadhotel.co.uk/

A former 18th century coaching inn.

Giggleswick School was founded in 1499 on half an acre of land leased by the Prior and Convent of Durham, to James Carr, the chantry priest at the Parish Church of St Alkelda, to enclose and build, at his own expense, one 'Gramar Scole'. The school was run by the chantry priests until Edward VI dissolved the position but was saved by the petition of the King's Chaplain, John Nowell, and in 1553 it received its royal charter. The charter granted land and endowed it with the title: The Free Grammar School of King Edward the VI of Giggleswick.

52. The Black Horse, Giggleswick

32 Church Street, Giggleswick, Settle BD24 0BE
01729 822506

A wonderful pub with numerous rooms all themed and replete with ornaments and decoration. The themes, to a large extent, mirror the licensees' lives and interests so, for example, there is a sports room, a military room and the main bar is populated with images and figures of Laurel and Hardy. There are ancient bagatelles on the walls and other old pub games. There is a gothic style façade and splendid stained glass windows. It is a pleasure to be in and to converse with the convivial owners.

The Quaker George Fox is reputed to have been imprisoned here around 1650 – shame he was a teetotaller.

Hospitable licensees at this 17th-c village pub prettily set by church; cosy bar with gleaming copper and brass, bric-a-brac and coal-effect fire, good value generously served food, well kept Timothy Taylors, Tetleys and guests, quick friendly service, intimate dining room; piano (often played), monthly quiz; children welcome till 9pm, no dogs (the resident doberman is Trevor), heated back terrace.

(thegoodpubguide.co.uk/pub/bd24+0be/black+horse/)

53. The Craven Heifer, Stainforth

Main Road, Stainforth, Settle BD24 9PB
01729 822435
www.cravenheiferstainforth.co.uk

A pleasing and homely pub next to Stainforth Beck in this pleasant village. There is a fine stained-glass window. The pub is popular with walkers – it is close to Pen-y-Ghent, Catrigg Force and Craven Lime Works, one of the largest industrial archaeology sites in the Dales.

54. Helwith Bridge Inn, Helwith Bridge

Helwith Bridge, Settle, North Yorkshire BD24 0EH
01729 860220
manager@helwithbridgeinn.co.uk
http://www.helwithbridgeinn.co.uk/

The building the Helwith Bridge Inn is now in dates back to the 1820s when it was built as a canteen for the local quarry workers. It has been a public house since the 1870s coinciding with the laying of the adjacent railway line. In the old school next to the Helwith Bridge Inn you will find the Yorkshire Subterranean Societies headquarters, which includes bunk facilities for up to forty people. The pub is the starting point of the Three Peaks cycle race.

Over the road from the Inn is the Helwith Bridge Fly Fishery. Helwith Bridge means bridge by the ford made of flat stones in Old Norse.

55. The Golden Lion, Horton

Nr Settle, North Yorkshire BD24 OHB
01729 860206
info@goldenlionhotel.co.uk

A former 16th century coaching inn. The building had been used as an outdoor centre before that and required extensive renovation before re-opening as a hotel in 1988. During the renovation an ancient well over 45 feet deep was discovered at the rear of the hotel. The well has been made into a feature.

56. The Crown, Horton

Hawes Road, Nr Settle, Horton In Ribblesdale, North Yorkshire BD24 0HF
01729 860209
http://www.crown-hotel.co.uk/

Ideally situated for both the Three Peaks and Pennine Way.

57. The Game Cock, Austwick

The Green, Austwick, Lancaster LA2 8BB
015242 51226
info@gamecockinn.co.uk
https://www.gamecockinn.co.uk/

Sports a fabulous, old-fashioned bar area decorated with cartoons and old photos of the pub and village. Popular with locals, hikers and cyclists – the pub is on National Cycle Network route 68 and the Way of the Roses.

Austwick means the dairy farm on the east side (Old Norse + Old English). The parish takes in the wonderfully named Wharfe, parts of Keasden, Feizor, Lawkland and Eldroth. A local folktale has it that when an Austwick man fell into a deep pool his friends could hear the words 'T' b-best's at t' b-bottom', so they too jumped into the pool, and were never seen again.

58. The New Inn, Clapham

Old Road, Clapham, North Yorkshire LA2 8HH
015242 51203
info@newinn-clapham.co.uk
www.newinn-clapham.co.uk

A capacious 18th century coaching inn, which features two lounge bars, the smaller with wood panelling.

The homestead on the noisy stream (Old English). Often called Clapham via Lancaster, as if there was a need to distinguish it from Clapham Junction. This Clapham is near to Trow Ghyll where a skeleton was found in August 1947 by two members of the Northern Pennine Club, Leach and (ironically) Burgess, looking for new pots to explore; they discovered a small hole (named Body Pot afterwards) partly covered by stones into which Leach climbed. He discovered a pair of shoes, then, looking round he saw the skull and the rest of the badly decomposed body; next to the body was a phial of white powder. The police were duly summoned and the remains taken to Skipton mortuary while the effects were sent to the forensic laboratory at Wakefield. By pure coincidence, a week later, another skeleton was found close by at Gaping Gill but this was a result of a fall into the cave two to three years previously.

The Body Pot post-mortem examination concluded that death had occurred at least two and no more than six years previously. None of the bones were broken or diseased, although some were missing, as was the brain. The phial contained sodium cyanide, a deadly poison, as did an ampule also found at the scene. There was also two pairs of shoes, a watch, handkerchief, studs, toothbrush, fountain pen, propelling pencil, compass, box of matches, tablets, flashlamp, and toiletries and a key. The verdict concluded that there was insufficient evidence of cause of death or to identify the remains. The historian A.W.B. Simpson, who happened to be living in Clapham at the time, reported that the only known users of such ampules were foreign spies operating undercover in enemy countries, who used them to commit suicide if necessary. Simpson suggested that the victim was 'plainly connected in some way with the German secret service'. He added enigmatically that 'Such enquiries as I have made from persons who ought to know have produced

evasiveness'. According to MI5, Germany had deployed around 115 agents in Britain during the war, most of whom had been identified and caught, with the exception of one, Willem Ter Braak, who had committed suicide before being captured. The identity of the skeleton remains a mystery.

There was another pub called the Flying Horseshoe at Clapham Station.

59. Clapham Cafe Bunk & Bar

(Formerly Reading Room; Clapham Bunk, Old Manor House)
Church Avenue, Clapham, Lancaster LA2 8EQ
015242 51144
www.claphambunk.com

Converted from the old manor house from 1620, this houses a bunkhouse and a café and bar with bare floorboards, bench seats and a small library. A huge fireplace dated 1701 accommodates a wood-burning stove.

Alan Bennett's early days in Armley, Leeds, define the man and inform much of his work. His regular forays over forty years to his house in the Dales village of Clapham further reinforce his associations with Yorkshire and add a rural landscape to the decidedly urban, working class and back-to-back backdrop that is Armley. Taken together, the rural and the urban merge to provide an influence that is unmistakably Yorkshire, with characters that are often decidedly northern, if not specifically Yorkshire, folk. His uncanny ear for Yorkshire dialect, the absurd and just plain daft things people sometimes say, office gossip minutiae, and the eccentricities of the ordinary man and woman is unmatched. His mother ('Mam') is a source of some of this with such axiomatic jewels as, on the trouble with being bald, was that 'You'd never know where to stop washing your face' – a gift that he elsewhere described as 'an unerring grasp of inessentials which is the prerogative of mothers'.

> *We have fish and chips, which W. and I fetch from the shop in Settle market-place. Some local boys come in and there is a bit of chat between them and the fish-fryer about whether the kestrel under the counter is for sale. … Only when I mention it to W. does he explain Kestrel is now a lager. I imagine the future is going to contain an increasing number of incidents like this, culminating with a man in a white coat saying to one kindly, 'And now can you tell me the name of the Prime Minister?'*

(Alan Bennett, *Writing Home* (1994) diary entry for 25 July 1985, p. 144)

60. Newby Head Inn

Newby Head is a mountain pass between Hawes and Ingleton, named after a drovers' inn, Newby Head Inn, which was the fourth highest inn in England. In January 1843, an inquest was held at the inn by the Skipton coroner with regard to Isaac Mason who had been found dead in bed. According to the landlord who was in the bed with him, he went downstairs to get a candle. When he returned he found Isaac Mason dead. The verdict was that Isaac died by the 'visitation of God'. Newby Head Pass is 1,439 ft (439 m) above sea level.

61. Three Horseshoes, Ingleton

41 Main Street, Ingleton, Carnforth LA6 3EH
015242 42370

62. Craven Heifer, Ingleton

1 Main Street, Ingleton, Carnforth LA6 3HG
015242 42515
www.cravenheiferingleton.co.uk

Converted from a row of terraces.

63. The Old Hill Inn, Chapel le Dale

Chapel-le-Dale, Ingleton, North Yorkshire LA6 3AR
015242 41256
info@oldhillinningleton.co.uk
http://www.oldhillinningleton.co.uk/enquiries.html

The Old Hill Inn dates back to 1615. Originally it was a farm, then a drovers' inn. Robert Southey and Turner visited.

Winston Churchill used to stay here for hunting and fishing holidays. The inn is used by hikers and potholers. Paths lead from here to both Whernside and Ingleborough.

Chapel le Dale is, literally, the chapel in the valley (Old French + Old English/Old Norse). It is close to the Ribblehead Viaduct, Great Douk Cave and the source of the River Doe.

64. The Station Inn, Ribblehead

Low Sleights Road, Ribblehead, Nr Ingleton, North Yorkshire LA6 3AS
015242 41274
info@stationinnribblehead.co.uk
www.stationinnribblehead.co.uk

Overlooks Settle and the breathtaking Ribblehead viaduct. It is a traditional 19th century country inn boasting real fires steeped in the history of the Settle to Carlisle Railway, the Ribblehead Viaduct, and Bleamoor Tunnel – three real icons all constructed by navvies living in the Jericho Settlement. Seven trains pass through Ribblehead each day between Leeds and Carlisle. Real ales are seasonal Tets Ales, only available here and specially brewed by Recoil.

The Station Inn is within one mile of the Dalesway walk on Ribbleway on the Dales highway. Also not far away are Whitescar Caves and Ingleton Waterfall.

> *Built at the same time as the nearby viaduct (1874). A welcome refuge in a bleak spot in the midst of superb walking country. Refurbished in 2017 to provide a rustic look throughout frequented by a surprisingly large number of locals. Good train service – times are above the bar counter – but buses rare (service threatened by funding cuts). Bunk barn next door, wild camping behind.*

(What?ub, 5 March 2018)

Work on the viaduct involved up to 2,300 men who lived onsite, often along with their families, in several shanty settlements with names such as Batty Wife Hole, Sebastopol, and Belgravia. One hundred or so workers died during the project, the majority

work accidents, fighting, or from outbreaks of smallpox. According to Church of England records, there are around 200 burials of men, women, and children in the graveyard at St Leonard's Chapel-le-Dale dating from the time of its construction; the church there has a memorial to the railway workers.

Ribblehead Viaduct stretches for 440 yards (400 m), and is 104 feet (32 m) above the valley floor at its highest point; it comprises twenty-four arches of 45 feet (14 m) span, the foundations of which are 25 feet (7.6 m) deep. The piers are tapered, being roughly 13 feet (4 m) across at the base and 5 feet 11 inches (1.8 m) thick near the arches with loosely packed rubble-filled cores. Every sixth pier is 50 per cent thicker, an intentional mitigating measure against complete collapse should any of the piers fail. The north end of the viaduct is 13 feet (4 m) higher than the south end resulting in a gradient of 1:100.

Batty Green nearby was one of the shanty towns built by workers on the Ribblehead viaduct. Batty Wife Cave was a deep pothole and the place where the Batty marriage came to a tragic end. Mr and Mrs Batty had separated after an argument but later agreed to meet up at the pothole and make up. When Mr Batty failed to show up his wife was so distraught she drowned herself in the hole – hence the name. An alternative version tells how Mr Batty murdered his wife after yet another argument.

Gearstones is the stony triangular plot of land (Old English) – near Ribblehead Viaduct. The earliest reference to the lodge here is 'Crossing a ford, Mr Blakey led me to a public house called Grierstones, the seat of misery in a desert ... wretched beer and brandy' – from the diaries of Lord Torrington in 1792. Not the best of recommendations.

SEDBERGH AND DENT

The Snooty Fox, Sun, King's Head and Red Lion– all in Kirkby Lonsdale

On the road from Tan Hill to Keld

65. The Red Dragon Inn, Kirkby Lonsdale

59–61 Main Street, Kirkby Lonsdale LA6 2AH
015242 71205

The view of the River Lune from the churchyard here is known as Ruskin's View; it was described by John Ruskin as 'One of the loveliest views in England' and painted by Turner.

Ruskin's View

66. Sun Hotel, Kirkby Lonsdale

Market Street, Kirkby Lonsdale LA6 2AU
015242 71965
www.sun-inn.info

A charming 17th century inn; in St Marys Churchyard you can still see the original sun dial which gave the inn its name.

67. The Snooty Fox, Kirkby Lonsdale

33 Main Street, Kirkby Lonsdale, LA6 2AH
015242 97298
www.snootyfoxtavern.co.uk/index

Kirkby Lonsdale is one of the few Cumbrian towns mentioned in the Domesday Book, where it is described as Cherchibi (village with a church). The earlier church was totally rebuilt by the Normans, who also erected an artificial motte on nearby glebe land. In later years, the mound was used for cockfighting, hence the current name of Cockpit Hill. In 1093, Ivo de Taillebois (Baron of Kendal) gifted the church at Kirkby Lonsdale to St Mary's Abbey in York.

68. Kings Arms Hotel, Kirkby Lonsdale

7 Market Street, Kirkby Lonsdale LA6 2AU
015242 71220

Kirkby Lonsdale's original and oldest inn, established in the 1500s. The working inglenook fireplace is reputedly the largest in Cumbria.

Mill Brow with its fast flowing stream was the industrial centre of Kirkby Lonsdale, with several water-powered mills for grinding corn, bark and bone, carding wool, manufacturing snuff, making bobbins, fulling cloth and sawing timber.

69. Royal Barn, Kirkby Lonsdale

New Road, Kirkby Lonsdale, Carnforth LA6 2AB
015242 71918
info@kirkbylonsdalebrewery.com
www.kirkbylonsdalebrewery.com

Tap house for Kirkby Lonsdale Brewery. The brewery slogan is: We put the 'ale' in Lonsdale!

Devil's Bridge dates from around 1370 and has three spans; at the eastern end is a sundial in the form of a square block on an octagonal column. The bridge was probably built by the monks of St Mary's Abbey, York; legend has it that the Devil appeared to an old woman, promising to build a bridge in exchange for the first soul to cross over it. When the bridge was finished, the woman threw bread over the bridge and her dog chased after it, thereby outwitting the Devil. Several large stones in the surrounding area, including the Great Stone of Fourstones, are ascribed to the Devil's purse-strings bursting open as he ferried masonry to build it.

70. The Pheasant Inn, Casterton

Casterton, Kirkby Lonsdale, Cumbria LA6 2RX
015242 71230
info@pheasantinn.co.uk
www.pheasantinn.co.uk

Casterton sits on the best part of the Three Counties System, the longest explored natural cave system in the UK.

71. The Barbon Inn, Barbon

Barbon, Nr Kirkby Lonsdale LA6 2LJ
01524 276233
info@barbon-inn.co.uk
https://www.barbon-inn.co.uk

Originally a farmhouse, this superb former coaching inn dates from around the 1650s.

This ancient bench dates from 1686 and was a wedding present from 'T' to 'H'.

72. Swan Inn, Middleton-in-Lonsdale

Middleton-in-Lonsdale LA6 2NB
015242 76223
www.swaninnmiddleton.co.uk/index.html

A 16th century coaching inn.

73. The Dalesman, Sedbergh

Main Street, Sedbergh LA10 5BN
015396 21183
www.thedalesman.co.uk

Formerly The Golden Lion.

Sedbergh can boast at least one house from the 14th century, and there are the remains of a motte and bailey castle thought to date from Saxon times. For many years Sedbergh's main industries were farming and the production of woollen garments. Wool was taken to mills where it was turned into yarn from which people knitted clothing, mainly hats and socks, in their homes. These garments were sold by local merchants to, among other places, the coal miners of the North East of England. This trade is recalled at Farfield Mill where there is an exhibition of weaving equipment, and workshops for a number of artists and crafts workers.

74. The Red Lion, Sedbergh

Finkle Street, Sedbergh, Cumbria LA10 5BZ
015396 20433

Sedbergh means a hill with a flat or seat-shaped top from Old Norse. Sedbergh is one England's book towns (along with Hay-on-Wye and Wigtown) with independent bookshops and dealers working out of the Dales & Lakes Book Centre, Sleepy Elephant, Old School Bookshop at Farfield Clothing, Clutterbooks, and Westwood Books.

75. George & Dragon, Dent

The George & Dragon Hotel, Main Street, Dent, Cumbria LA10 5QL
01539 625 256
www.thegeorgeanddragondent.co.uk

A Grade 2 listed building overlooking the famous Adam Sedgwick Memorial Fountain. Brewery tap for Dent Brewery. Dent means the hill, probably from Old Irish 'dind'.

Standing in the Market Place in the village of Dent is an impressive Shap granite monument. The memorial fountain commemorates the life and work of Adam Sedgwick [1785–1873) who was one of the founders of modern geology. A distinguished mathematician, clergyman and geologist, Sedgwick was born in the village in 1785. After his education at Dent School and Sedbergh Grammar school, Sedgwick went on to Trinity College, Cambridge, where he graduated with a first class honours in mathematics in 1808. He was appointed a fellow of Trinity College in 1810 and was ordained in 1817, going on to become a canon in Norwich cathedral. Sedgwick was appointed Woodwardian Professor of Geology at Cambridge in 1819 and in 1823, he made a detailed study of rocks in the Lake District. In 1829 Sedgwick became President of the Geological Society of London. Charles Darwin studied geology under Sedgwick at Cambridge before departing on the Beagle in 1831 as project naturalist. The memorial was erected by the people of Dent in the late 19th century and is inscribed with Sedgwick's name in Gothick lettering.

(https://ahistoricalhiatus.com/2016/06/28/dent-adam-sedgwick-memorial-fountain/)

76. Sun Inn, Dent

Main Street, Dent LA10 5QL
015396 25208
martin@dalecom.co.uk
www.suninndent.co.uk

According to What?ub:

> *A typical dales village inn at the top of Dent's cobbled main street. This 300 year old inn has no modern distractions but offers a warm welcome and open fires … with wooden floors, traditional bench seating and wooden stools and armchairs.*

Dent station is the highest mainline station in England and part of the Settle–Carlisle railway. There are superb viaducts at Dent Head and Arten Gill.

77. The Sportsman's Inn, Cowgill

Cowgill LA10 5RG
015396 25282
info@thesportsmaninn.com
www.thesportsmansinn.com

The 17th century Grade II listed building dates back over 350 years and, in its time, has served the drovers taking livestock to the nearby market towns and navvies working on the Settle Carlisle railway line.

Cowgill means the dam in the ravine from a dialect word 'caul' meaning dam or weir and Old Norse.

78. The Moorcock Inn, Garsdale Head

Sedbergh, Cumbria LA10 5PU
01969 667488
moorcockinn@outlook.com
www.moorcockinn.com

For train enthusiasts the Moorcock Inn is pure heaven because they can see the nearby Dandry Mire/Moorcock Viaduct from the pub with its twelve arches. It stands 50 feet high and is 227 yards long.

Garsdale means Garth's valley (Old Norse personal name + Old Norse/Old English).

The Moorcock Inn is 400 yards (365 m) east from the border with Cumbria and 1,476 yards (1,500 m) north-east from Garsdale railway station, previously Hawes Junction. The Moorcock Inn dates to the 1740s. East of the inn towards Garsdale station is Dandry Mire Viaduct (or Moorcock Viaduct). On Christmas Eve 1910, the St Pancras to Glasgow Express collided into the back of two engines while passing over the viaduct. The twelve dead from the crash were kept in the Moorcock's cellar before burial in Hawes churchyard.

The inn, about 1900

THE LUNE VALLEY AND WESTMORLAND DALES

79. Black Swan, Ravenstonedale

Ravenstonedale, Kirkby Stephen, Cumbria CA17 4NG
015396 23204
enquiries@blackswanhotel.com
http://www.blackswanhotel.com/index.html

Ravenstonedale was also known as 'Russendale'; the parish is divided into four parts ('angles'): Town, Newbiggin-on-Lune, Bowderdale and Fell End. An alternative spelling is Rausyngdale.

80. King's Head, Ravenstonedale

Ravenstonedale, Kirkby Stephen, Cumbria CA17 4NH
015396 23050
enquiries@kings-head.com
http://www.kings-head.com/

Dating from the 16th century, the King's Head is a Grade II listed whitewashed building.

81. The Fat Lamb, Ravenstonedale

Crossbank, Ravenstonedale, Kirkby Stephen, Cumbria CA17 4LL
015396 23242
enquiries@fatlamb.co.uk
http://www.fatlamb.co.uk/

What?ub tells us:

Front bar is cosy with wooden floor and an old black cooking stove that provides additional heating when cold. Look for the sheep cartoons to the left of the stove. To the right of the bar is a quaint small carpeted parlour complete with wooden writing desk. Look into the room to the right and see evidence of the owner's love of vintage cars; there is a selection of memorabilia including dozens of model cars.

82. Black Bull, Nateby

Nateby CA17 4JP
017683 71588
www.nateby-inn.co.uk

83. The Kings Arms Hotel, Kirkby Stephen

Market Square, Kirkby Stephen CA17 4QN
017683 72906
kingsarmshotelkirkbystephen.co.uk

A 17th century coaching inn. Kirkby Stephen Grammar School was founded in 1566 by Thomas Wharton, 1st Baron Wharton, under letters patent granted by Queen Elizabeth I.

84. Pennine Hotel, Kirkby Stephen

Market Square, Kirkby Stephen CA17 4QT
017683 71382
penninehotel.com

In 1352–1353 Roger de Clifford, Baron of Westmorland, obtained a charter from King Edward III, for a market and two yearly fairs to be held in the town. This was reaffirmed by a charter granted in 1605 to George, Earl of Cumberland, by King James I, for: 'one market on Monday and two fairs yearly; one on the Wednesday, Thursday and Friday after Whitsuntide and the other on the two days next before the feast of St. Luke'.

Travellers on their way to Appleby Fair through Kirkby Stephen in June 2018.

85. White Lion, Kirkby Stephen

4 Market Street, Kirkby Stephen CA17 4QS
017683 71481
roytaylor55@hotmail.com

The Nine Standards

Every June 'Mallerstang Horseshoe and Nine Standards Yomp' is held, which goes along both sides of the neighbouring dale of Mallerstang, including Wild Boar Fell and the summit of nearby Nine Standards. Nine Standards Rigg is to the north-east, Pendragon Castle and Wild Boar Fell, to the south. Legend has it that the castle was built by Uther Pendragon, father of King Arthur, who is said to have unsuccessfully tried to divert the river to provide its moat.

Uther was probably a 5th century chieftain who led resistance to the invading Anglo-Saxons. According to another local legend, Uther and many of his men died here when the Saxons poisoned the well.

86. Black Bull, Kirby Stephen

38 Market Street, Kirkby Stephen, CA17 4QW
017683 71237
blackbullkirkbystephen.co.uk

87. Bay Horse Inn, Winton

Winton CA17 4HS
017683 71451
thebayhorsewinton.co.uk

SWALEDALE AND ARKENGARTHDALE

Dale of the rushing river (Old English). Reputedly the fastest-flowing in England.

Between Low Row and Askrigg

88. Tan Hill Inn

Tan Hill Inn, Reeth, Richmond DL11 6ED
01833 628 246
info@tanhillinn.com
www.tanhillinn.com/

The Tan Hill Inn is the highest inn in the UK at 1,732 feet (528 m) above sea level. The building originates from the 17th century and during the 18th century was used by workers working nearby in the coal pits, and packhorse drovers, or jaggers. At this time the pub was known

Unknown ballerina behind the bar

as The Kings Pit. The last mine on Tan Hill closed in 1929, although the pub survived on the custom from local farmers and the increased reach of visitors in the new-fangled motor car. The building is noted for its isolation, but it used to be surrounded by miners' cottages, until these were knocked down after the closure of the mines in the 1920s.

Snow ploughs at the ready

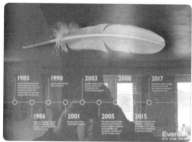

The guilty feather

Television adverts, if nothing else, have helped to make Tan Hill famous with its unique position, apparent desolation and its unrivalled ambience. Ted Moult's 'Everest' Double Glazing advert (featuring the floating feather) from the 1980s and in the late 1990s the 'Vodafone' adverts featuring the 'Wolf & Whistle' pub have been the real stars in Tan Hill's film career. You can see the actual window and feather above the bar.

In 2008 'Everest' went back and refitted the windows and doors and installed solar panels.

Sadly, the 'Wolf & Whistle' adverts encouraged the use of mobiles in the pub so the only solution was to crack down on their use: pickled phones can be seen in a jar – 'pay a 50p fine or in they go!'

Less well known is the fact that in 1995 Tan Hill became the first pub in the UK to hold a licence for marriage ceremonies.

Tan Hill Inn has featured in *Robin Hood Prince of Thieves* and the 'Harry Potter' films, *It Shouldn't Happen To A Vet*, *The Inspector Lindley Mysteries*, *Murder in Mind*,

Top Gear, The Fast Show, Wish You Were Here, All Creatures Great and Small and *Jude the Obscure.*

In 2009 New Year's Eve celebrants were the luckiest ever to be snowed-in; they were unable to leave the pub for three days.

The wireless was a novelty at the inn in 1930 and Susan Peacock, the landlady, would participate in frequent radio broadcasts, waxing lyrical about the quiet life up there. This increased further the popularity of the pub with hundreds of people visiting.

Coal mining on Tan Hill goes back at least to the 14th century and maybe earlier. The earliest records of coal being produced exist from 1384, when shallow shafts excavated coal for Richmond Castle. By the 17th century the poor-quality coal was converted in simple beehive kilns into coke – known locally as 'cinders' – which was used in lead and iron smelting. The coal was a poor quality crow coal known for the soot it gave off when burnt, and useless for firing steam engines – where later the real demand and money was. But '... *many a farm wife preferred the small dusty outcrop coal which when mixed with peat, burns with a heating glow and can be banked up at night, and with a little poking, made bright as ever in the morning'*. Crow coal was used to fuel the lime kilns of Arkengarthdale – an environmental catastrophe because of the pollution and because the wood burning kilns led to the stripping of Swaledale of its trees. Less damagingly, horses would line up with their carts waiting to be loaded with coal for Reeth and other parts of Swaledale while the miners would sing and get drunk in the pub.

The AdoptaPub website tells us:

> Tan Hill Inn certainly had its share of licensees. The longest serving was
> Susan Peacock who ran the pub between the two World Wars. She was
> born in the pub and local legend has it that she is buried behind it. During
> that time the inn was a rough place and fisticuffs would often break out
> between the miners ... Susan Peacock kept a loaded pistol behind the bar
> for such occasions … Many bits and pieces from that history, particularly
> from Susan Peacock's reign as landlady, may be viewed at Swaledale Folk
> Museum in Reeth … There was (and still is) no mains electricity … There
> are some pubs that are respected beyond bricks, mortar and beer. There
> are some pubs that are institutions, that bond thousands of people from
> all over the country. Tan Hill is one such pub.

(http://www.sunriseag.net/adoptapub/more/0019TanHill.htm)

89. Keld Lodge, Keld

Keld, Nr Richmond, North Yorkshire DL11 6LL
01748 886259
info@keldlodge.com
www.keldlodge.com

Originally built as a shooting lodge in 1860, Keld Lodge has been open as a hotel, bar
and restaurant since 2007 when it was converted from a youth hostel. Keld is where
the Pennine Way and Coast to Coast path meet. It opened at Easter 2007 to become
Keld's first pub since temperance campaigners bought and closed the Cat Hole Inn in
1954. The Cat Hole was similarly remote in a Tan Hill sort of way and has been called
'the loneliest inn in the world' and 'the last outpost of civilisation'. It changed its
name to the Miners Arms but reverted to Cat Hole when the mining boom was over.

Keld derives from the Viking word Kelda meaning a spring. The place was once
called AppletreKelde – the spring near the apple trees. The ruins of Crackpot Hall
are a mile east of Keld. The current ruinous Crackpot Hall is a farmhouse dating
from the mid-18th century. It was a fine two-storey building with a slate roof and

matching 'shippons' or cow sheds at each end for animals. The building may also have been used as lead mine offices.

In the heyday of the lead-mining industry in Swaledale in the late 19th century, the village could boast a population of around 6,000. During this time a number a of impressive buildings – now Grade II listed – were built: they include the Congregational and Methodist chapels, the school and the Literary Institute.

90. Farmers Arms, Muker

The Farmers Arms, Muker, Richmond, North Yorkshire DL11 6QG
01748 886297
enquiries@farmersarmsmuker.co.uk
www.farmersarmsmuker.co.uk

From the website: at last a pub and description that are devoid of the usual platitudes and clichés, and tells it how it is; oh that others take note:

> *We do not take bookings (apart from NYE) but operate a first come first served basis as pubs always used to. If there are no tables available when you arrive, you'll be placed in a table queue – and if you're happy to share tables and meet new folk, then we can get you seated even quicker – you may even make new friends. It's what pubs are about, socialising and meeting new people. That is why we don't take kindly to prominent use of laptops, iPads, children's video games or indiscreet use of mobile phones – they all detract from the traditional pub atmosphere and the art of conversation. This way of thinking may not appeal to everyone, and we apologise to those we may offend by not giving out our 'WEP' key or reserving tables.*

Muker is from the Viking mjor-aker (acre) meaning a small piece of land. In 1274 it was Meuhaker. One former landlady was Old Nanny Peacock, possibly a relative of Tan Hill's Susan Peacock.

Nearby Thwaite is a Viking name for meadow – thveit. In 1301 it was personalised to Arkeltwayt and became Arkle's wood. There are two Yorkshire Angrams: one near Muker, the other near Harrogate. Angr is an old word for grazing land. The original name would have been Angrum, plural form of Angr. Angram Reservoir is the first of three reservoirs you come to on the River Nidd in Upper Nidderdale; the others are Scar House Reservoir and Gouthwaite Reservoir.

There was another pub here: The Queens Arms; the publican in 1893 was William Peacock. There also used to be a pub in Thwaite: The Joiners Arms; the publican in 1893 was Ralph Alderson, a local farmer.

91. Kings Head, Gunnerside

Reeth DL11 6LD
01748 886261
info@kingsheadgunnerside.com
www.kingsheadgunnerside.com

A small two-room pub that was formerly a 17th century blacksmith's. Gunnerside is a Viking name meaning Gunnar's slope. Local commerce focuses on clockmaking, hill farming, gamekeeping and the maintenance of traditional stone-built field walls, houses and barns.

Meadows and barn near Gunnerside

92. Punch Bowl Inn, Low Row

Low Row, Richmond, North Yorkshire DL11 6PF
01748 886945
info@pbinn.co.uk
http://www.pbinn.co.uk/

Robert Thompson's mice inhabit the bar of this inn dating from 1638. Pubs named Punch Bowl often denoted a Whig establishment and their patrons' predilection for punch; the Tories still preferred their port and red wines.

The name Low Row derives from the Norse 'The Wra' (a nook). The surname 'Raw' has associations with the village, which was raided by Jacobites in 1745, and bodies probably from that raid are buried at the church here, Low Row United Reformed Church.

Nearby is Crackpot: nothing eccentric about this derivation. In 1298 Crackpot was called Crakepot, the name deriving from the Old English 'Kraka', a crow and the Viking word 'Pot' – often a deep hole in a river bed, but in Crackpot's case it refers to a rift in the limestone. This meaning of pot also crops up in Potto near Swainby, Sand Pot near Northallerton and in Pot Hall and the Pot Beck near Masham. The word is still used in Swedish today. There is a Crackpot Hall near Keld.

There was another pub here: The Queens Arms; the publican in 1893 was Edmund Coates, an auctioneer and local farmer.

93. The Buck, Reeth

Reeth, Swaledale, Richmond, North Yorkshire DL11 6SW
01748 884210
buckhotelreeth@gmail.com
www.buckhotel.co.uk/index

The Buck was originally a coaching inn dating from around 1760, located at the centre of the village where a toll was charged to passing travellers. Original features include an ancient beamed ceiling adorned with an interesting array of horse brass, an ice house and strange door knockers.

Reeth is from an Anglo Saxon word meaning at the stream. At one time it was a centre for hand-knitting and the local lead in upper Swaledale. During World War II the old school building was used to billet troops attending the six week Battle Training Camp at Catterick. Recent restoration work uncovered tins of boot polish and anti-gas ointment along with packets of Navy Cut and Woodbine cigarettes under the floorboards.

Nearby Healaugh means the clearing in the high forest (Old English from Heah). The village telephone box is unusually well furnished, with a carpet, waste paper bin, ash tray, directories and fresh flowers. Visitors are encouraged to leave a donation. Here, Healaugh Park Priory is now called Healaugh Manor Farm, founded in 1218 by Jordan de Santa Maria and his wife, Alice, who was the granddaughter of Betram Haget who had granted the lands for a hermitage to Gilbert, a monk from Marmoutier.

94. The Black Bull, Reeth

High Row, Reeth DL11 6SZ
01748 884213
ratkinson@blackbull104.wanadoo.co.uk
www.theblackbullreeth.co.uk

The Black Bull is the oldest of the three pubs here dating from 1680; it is famous for its upside-down sign – inverted after a dispute with National Park authorities over the pub's external rendering, and remains so today. The King's Arms, or 'Middle House' goes back to 1734.

From the website:

> *Why is the Black Bull sign upside down?*
>
> *Bob Sykes, a previous landlord of the Black Bull was more than surprised when National Parks officials took exception to his attempts to tidy up the exterior of the public house. He removed the render from the outside of the hotel to expose the original 250-year-old walls. The work was partly carried out to comply with English Tourist Board accommodation grading requirements.*

But Mr Sykes also feared that the crumbling render was a potential danger to the public. However, Park officials threatened legal action if the render was not replaced. The Authorities argued that the building would originally have had some form of render. Shortly after the render was removed, some local pranksters turned the sign upside down in protest at the Authorities attitude. The sign has moved now but still remains upside down.

Good on Bob Sykes and people like him...

Reeth had three strings to its commercial bow: it became a centre for hand-knitting and the local lead industry was controlled from here; at the same time it always was a market centre for the local farming community. Alfred Wainwright's Coast to Coast Walk, from Saint Bees to Robin Hood's Bay, passes through Reeth.

95. Kings Arms, Reeth

High Row, Reeth DL11 6SY
01748 884259
enquiries@thekingsarms.com
www.thekingsarms.com

One Man and his Dog

Typical of Lucie Hinson's work, this is an evocative picture of a Dales shepherd and his dog in Reeth in the 1950s.

© Lucie Hinson

It was the Cistercians, Premonstratensians and Gilbertines who developed the sheep farming and resultant woollen industry in and around Richmond from around the 12th century. This was eventually taken over by the Company of the Merchants of the Staple in the 15th century; all wool had to pass through the Woolhouse for weighing (in the Tollbooth) and could only be sold from there. Around 1620 the government recognised Richmond as a Staple Town along with Leeds and Ripon. In 1664 we know that 2,000 dozen pairs of stockings were exported via Stockton, appropriately enough.

96. The Bridge Inn, Grinton

Grinton, Reeth DL11 6HH
01748 884224
atkinbridge@btinternet.com
www.bridgeinn-grinton.co.uk

The Bridge Inn – a former coaching inn dating back to the 13th century – lies beneath the glowering Fremington Edge and Harkerside on both the Coast-to-Coast and Inn Way walks, and the Dales Cycle Way. It is opposite the church of St Andrew, known as the 'Cathedral of the Dales' and goes back to the 12th century, founded by William de Ghent, a relative of William the Conqueror. The church is the principal church for the whole of upper Swaledale, with burials coming from far and wide. The bodies were carried as much as sixteen miles down the valley along the footpath from Keld, now known as the Corpse Way or Corpse Road, in wicker coffins. A number of long stones, located at intervals along the path, traditionally called 'coffin stones', are where the coffins would have been set down while the pallbearers took a break.

Observant visitors will have noticed the sheep and guitar on the pub's chimney; sculptor Mike Kutz replaces the instrument every year (always a last-minute secret) to coincide with the start of each Swaledale Festival. Previous years have featured a French horn and a cornet – someone stole the cornet. Licensee Andrew Atkin tells an eye-watering story about the positioning of the French horn – not publishable here.

© Lucie Hinson

Sheep Shearing at Grinton Smelt Mill

This isn't as bad as it looks. Lucie Hinson's 1950s photograph neatly captures Swaledale's two main industries: lead mining and wool. The buildings here comprise a peat store and smelting furnaces. The toxic lead fumes were dispelled through the flue, which originally joined the smelting building and still goes up the hillside to the top of Sharrow Hill. Over the years stone has been quarried from the furnaces while farmers have requisitioned the buildings and have made a sheep dip.

97. Red Lion, Langthwaite

Langthwaite, Richmond, North Yorkshire DL11 6RE
01748 884218
www.redlionlangthwaite.co.uk

Another veteran of *All Creatures Great and Small* from 1977 to 1991 when the inside and the exterior of the Red Lion was used in several episodes.

Other starring roles were in *A Woman of Substance* and the sequel *Hold the Dream* starring Deborah Kerr, Jenny Seagrove, Nigel Havers and Paul Daneman, and *Escape from the Dark* starring Maurice Coleman and Alistair Sim.

98. Charles Bathurst Inn, Langthwaite

Arkengarthdale, Richmond, North Yorkshire DL11 6EN
01748 884567
info@cbinn.co.uk
http://www.cbinn.co.uk/about/

Also known as The CB Inn. Takes its short name from Charles Bathurst – 18th century lord of the manor and lead mine owner whose lead pigs are all stamped with his initials, like the 1750 pub. An ancestor, Dr John Bathurst, was Oliver Cromwell's physician. The Duke of Norfolk's shooting lodge is nearby, and the pub sports a quintessentially English quoits pitch.

The local church is the gothic revival St Marys in Arkengarthdale. It came about in the early 19th century when the area needed a new church to administer to the spiritual needs of an influx of lead miners. The 'Waterloo' church, one of 600 to be built after the battle, is unusual because the parts were all imported from London. Even rarer is a cast-iron gravestone – for iron founder Thomas Barningham, who died in 1843.

The area is a delightful treasure trove of fascinating and intriguing names: the moors are sprinkled with dilapidated lead mines from the 18th and 19th centuries amongst which is Surrender Bridge and Old Gang Lead Smelting Mill. Then there

A big night out in Booze.

is the so apt (for this book) hamlet of Booze, a narrow valley called Slei Gill, Bouldershaw Hill and Arkle Beck.

Arkengarthdale is a dale running north-west to south-east from Swaledale at Reeth, and is the northernmost of the Yorkshire Dales, Arkengarthdale means Arkle's enclosure in the valley, Arkle being a common Viking personal name. Garth is Viking for an enclosure; the dale is formed by the Arkle Beck: the unclassified road at Reeth crosses a number of other becks such as Great Punchard Gill, Roe Beck, Annaside Beck, and William Gill. It passes through Raw, Arkle Town, Langthwaite (from where a back road leads to Booze), Eskeleth and Whaw.

The 1851 census records 1,283 people living in the dale, 1,073 of which were born there. Males comprised 659; 254 of whom were lead miners and a further forty-two worked in smelting, construction and transportation. Eighteen women and children washed the ore. There were seven coal miners in William Gill and forty-nine farms employing sixty-four men and women. Of the fourteen trades counted there were four dressmakers, one knitter and one tailor. Fifty-one of the 294 boys under the age 15, and forty of the 247 girls attended school. Thirty-seven men from Arkengarthdale served in World War I, three of whom were killed. 1921 was the first year in which anyone in the dale owned a car, a Ford.

Arkle, as noted above, is a Norse personal name and probably came here with settlers during the 10th century. It once had a parish church, inn and workhouse. In the 19th century a lead ingot stamped with the name Hadrian (the Roman emperor from ad 117 to 138) was found, at Hurst, to the east of the dale. This, combined with records of the Romans at Richmond using Brigantian slaves to dig for lead, suggests that the Romans were mining lead in Arkengarthdale in the 2nd century. The plethora of Viking names, including Fagger Gill, Kitley Hill, Langthwaite and Whaw, indicates that the Vikings were around during the 10th century.

Booze was afflicted by a tragedy during the 18th century when miners underground near Boldershaw blasted into an underground lake. Twenty-four miners and two pit ponies were drowned; eighteen of the dead came from Booze. The seam became known as the Water Blast Vein. The interesting name of Booze comes from Old English boga and hus, making 'the house by the bend' – a reference either to the bend in the nearby beck or a curve on hillside. It is called Bowehouse in 1473.

The remote hamlet of Hurst had a Green Dragon that would have vied with Tan Hill for its desolation. It served the lead miners which date as far back as the 2nd century ad.

99. The George & Dragon, Hudswell

North Yorkshire DL11 6BL
01748 518373
info@georgeanddragonhudswell.com
www.georgeanddragonhudswell.co.uk/community-pub

The website proclaims:

> *Award winning real ale pub serving proper pies*
> *2016 CAMRA National Pub of the Year*
> *2017 & 2016 CAMRA Yorkshire Pub of the Year*
> *2018 & 2017 & 2016 CAMRA North West Yorkshire*
>   *Pub of the Year*
> *2017 Yorkshire Life food & drink awards pub of the Year*

When Hudswell's only pub, The George and Dragon, closed in 2008, the villagers didn't just sit there, glasses empty, and moan – they got off their bar stools and founded Hudswell Community Pub Ltd in December 2009, as an Industrial and Provident Society (an IPS Cooperative) for the benefit of the community.

By February 2010, 140 people had responded to the first call for investors and the associated prospectus and the initial target of £220,000 of investment was achieved – HCP duly completed the purchase of the George and Dragon pub.

Additional investors plus grant aid brought the total to £300,000 which enabled a major refurbishment project and several modifications to the building and bar area to be undertaken.

The pub was finally re-opened by then Foreign Secretary and HCP member, William Hague on 12 June 2010. The phrase 'The Pub is the Hub' was coined by HRH The Prince of Wales who, through his Princes Countryside Fund, was looking to raise the awareness of the value of the village pub to its community. In September 2015 the George and Dragon and HCP hosted a visit from the Prince. it now offers its own library, shop, allotments and various other community facilities as well as food and drink.

> *Paul Ainsworth, from Camra, said the George & Dragon was a 'great example of how a pub has been resurrected as a true community asset. To go from closed doors to winning national Pub of the Year in just a few short years is a fantastic achievement for any pub – and all the more impressive for one that is cooperatively owned. The story of the George & Dragon goes to show that in the right hands a closed pub can become viable and successful. We are very impressed with the work the community group has undertaken to save their local and hope that other communities are encouraged by the example when faced with an ongoing battle to save their own local.'*
>
> (Paul Ainsworth, Camra's Pub of the Year finalist coordinator,
> https://www.georgeanddragonhudswell.co.uk/community-pub)

100. The Bolton Arms, Downholme

Downholme, Richmond, North Yorkshire DL11 6AE
01748 823716
www.boltonarmsdownholme.com

Until recently, The Bolton Arms, formerly the Bolton Inn, was the only pub in England owned by Her Majesty the Queen, as it was formerly owned by the Ministry of Defence. The Bolton Arms was bought by the MoD in the 1930s to serve servicemen and women on exercise in the surrounding military training area. At one time the MoD owned the village of Downholme, but in 2012 it sold off its last remaining homes and a farmhouse in the community.

There used to be a second pub in Downholme called The King's Head, which closed in 1911.

In Richmond's Bridge Street at Green Bridge (now a private house), The Bridge was originally called The Tile Sheds Inn. Its claim to be the oldest pub in England (proudly painted on the front wall of the pub at one time) may be a little exaggerated. At one time, Richmond had sixty pubs. These included such exotically named houses as The Cleaver, or Chopping Knife; Dainty Davy (a racehorse); The Gaping Goose and The Bishop Blaize, formerly called The Elephant. This last one underlines the importance of wool to the town and to Swaledale – Bishop Blaize being the patron saint of woolcombers. Blaize was Bishop of Sebasta in Armenia and was martyred in 316 AD. In 1921 Richmond also had two temperance Hotels, both in Market Place: Varey's and The Albany.

Some of Richmond's lost pubs with date of closure where known, from http://www.closedpubs.co.uk/yorkshire/richmond.html:

Board Inn, 13 Bargate.
Bridge, Bridge Street.
Brewery Inn, The Green.
Golden Lion 2011, Market Place.
Good Intent 1913, Sleegill. Now in residential use.
Kings Arms 1813, King Street. Demolished.
Lass of Richmond Hill.
Oak Tree, Bridge Street. Publican in 1893 was
 Mary Gates.

Punch Bowl, Market Place.
Red Lion, Finkle Street.
Richmond Hotel, Market Place.
Ship, Frenchgate.
Three Tuns, Bargate.
Wellington Inn, Market Place. The publican in 1893 was Mary Trotter.

101. The Good Intent Inn, Richmond

A fascinating piece of pub theatre at The Good Intent in Sleegill, now a private house.

Drinkers in and around Richmond through the 19th century up to World War I showed immense passion in their support of the local, and the patrons of The Good Intent Inn were no exception. Here, we see a group of regulars bedecked in mayoral

regalia playing out the annual ceremony of electing a mayor – in imitation of the civic ceremony held in Richmond. The winner received a parchment outlining his duties along with a battered tin to symbolise the chains of office. Other enthusiasts in other pubs included Newbigginers in the Buck, Frenchgate Headers in the Ship, Greeners in the Bridge and Brewery and Bargaters in the Board and Oak Tree.

102. King's Head, Richmond

Market Place, Richmond DL10 4HS
01748 850220
http://www.kingsheadrichmond.co.uk

The large three-storey Georgian building on the left is The King's Head; according to What?ub: 'a very plush hotel in centre of town with a menu to match; this is the place to go for a spot of old-fashioned comfort'.

A portrait that hangs there is reputedly of Frances I'Anson – the subject of the song 'Lass of Richmond Hill' written by the lawyer and sometime poet Leonard McNally whom she later married. The hotel in the pre-World War days featured a ladies' drawing room, a coffee room, private suites and a garage with a shuttle bus to meet trains arriving at the station. Performing pigs entertained guests in the pleasure garden (Plasingdale Gardens) where there was also a bowling green and a cock pit.

It was originally built as a gentleman's townhouse in 1717 for the Bathhurst family, whose wealth came from lead mining; the ballroom where Franz Liszt performed is still there. Other guests include J.M.W. Turner who described the hotel as 'the finest in Richmondshire'. Feedback to die for. John Byng, Viscount Torrington, stayed there in 1792 but was not 'highly gratify'd' with his dinner: 'stale salmon and butter'd chops that did not make my chops water!' After his meal he went for a walk to Easby Abbey, and on returning to The King's Head helped himself from the larder to 'a cold shoulder of lamb … a gooseberry pie … and a good bottle of port'. He surmised that he 'never dealt better'.

Rumour has it that the younger Charles Bathurst 'chucked' a waiter down the staircase at the inn causing him to break his leg. When the innkeeper protested, Bathurst retorted, 'put it on the bill'. The king on the sign of The King's Head honoured King Charles II (1660–1685) rather than the reigning monarch at the time the inn was built, George I (1714–1727).

Cock fighting at the pit behind The King's Head was a main attraction for the nobility and gentry, and was associated with the town's horse racing meetings, as described in the *Newcastle Courant* in June 1731, promoting a three-day meeting at Richmond from 30 June to 2 July. Prize money was between £15 and £30, and on the morning of each race-day there would be a cock fighting match 'at Mr John Heslop's at the sign of The King's Head … betwixt the Gentlemen of Richmond and the Gentlemen of Bedale, showing 25 cocks each side, for two guineas a battle, and 20 guineas the main, or odd battle'.

103. Shoulder of Mutton, Richmond

Kirby Hill, Richmond, North Yorkshire DL11 7JH
01748 905011
shoulderofmutton481@gmail.com
www.shoulderofmutton.net

104. Unicorn Inn, Richmond

2 Newbiggin, Richmond, DL10 4DT
01748 822192

105. Bishop Blaize Hotel, Richmond

Market Place, Richmond DL10 4QL
01748 518087
bishopblaize@live.com
www.bishopblaize.co.uk

WENSLEYDALE

Wensleydale means the valley with Waendel's woodland clearing (Old English personal name + Old English + Old Norse). Unusually named after a village and not the river. Sometimes called Yoredale.

Above Askrigg

106. The Green Dragon, Hardraw

Hardraw, Hawes DL8 3LZ
01969 667392
www.greendragonhardraw.com

This quaint 13th century inn is one of the most charming pubs in the Yorkshire Dales. Standing at the entrance to the

impressive Hardraw Force, visitors to the waterfall must first pass through the Green Dragon, many of them returning for a couple of pints after the walk. Inside, it is dark and cosy with low-beamed ceilings and open fires taking you back in time.

Hardraw Force means the shepherds' row of cottages (Old English) + ON fors, foss. It is also spelt Hardrow; 1606 saw it as Hardrawe. This is England's largest single drop waterfall at 100 foot and is in the grounds of the Green Dragon Inn.

Turner and Wordsworth visited the waterfall; both stayed at the Green Dragon Inn.

107. Simonstone Hall Hotel, Hardraw

Hardraw, Hawes DL8 3LY
01969 667255
www.simonstonehall.com

> *The land upon which Simonstone stands was once a part of a larger empire owned by the Abbots of Jervaulx. Used mainly as grazing land for their renowned breed of horses, the area supported a small farm building – the earliest ancestor of Simonstone Hall.*
>
> (Franko Mutinelli, manager and part owner of Simonstone Hall Hotel, www.simonstonehall.com)

108. The Crown, Hawes

Market Place, Hawes DL8 3RD
01969 667212
crownhawes@gmail.com
www.crownhawesltd.co.uk

Hawes derives from the old Norse hals – a narrow neck of land (between mountains). Hawes was the home of Kit Calvert (1903–1984), the saviour of Wensleydale cheese: in 1935 he turned the Wensleydale Creamery at Hawes into a farmers' cooperative when it was threatened with closure.

> *Kit Calvert, saviour of Wensleydale Cheese in the 1930s, was recorded in 1979 telling the tale of his life, in his own words, as a young man before*

the First World War. The eldest son of a quarryman in Burtersett, Kit recalls his parents trying to raise a family of three on 18 shillings a week (90p). They survived by keeping their own geese and hens, although many of the eggs were sold to eke out their weekly income. Kit recollects asking his mother if he could eat a whole egg, rather than one half, to be told 'Half an egg was good enough for David Lloyd George!'

(W.R. Mitchell Archive, http://www.wrmitchellarchive.org.uk/node/57)

109. The Board Inn, Hawes

Market Place, Hawes DL8 3RD
01969 667223
ann@theboardinn.co.uk
www.theboardinn.co.uk

Pubs named 'The Board' tend to indicate that cold meats were on offer inside – the board being what the meats were served on, hence 'board and lodge'.

We have French Cistercian monks from the Roquefort region, who had settled in Wensleydale, to thank for Wensleydale cheese. Around 1150 they built a monastery at Fors, but later moved to Jervaulx in Lower Wensleydale. They came bearing a recipe for making cheese from sheep's milk. During the 14th century, cows' milk was used instead, slowly changing the character of the cheese. A soupçon of ewes' milk was still used in the mix in since it gave a more open texture, and allowed the development of the blue mould. At that time, Wensleydale was almost always blue with the white variety almost unknown. Nowadays, the opposite is true. When the monastery was dissolved in 1540, the local farmers continued making the cheese until World War II, during which most milk in the country was used for the making of 'Government Cheddar'.

110. The Fountain, Hawes

Market Place, Hawes DL8 3RD
01969 667206
enquiries@fountainhawes.co.uk
www.fountainhawes.co.uk

Wensleydale Creamery in Hawes has been hand-making cheese for more than 100 years. In May 1992, Dairy Crest, a subsidiary of the Milk Marketing Board, closed the

Hawes creamery with the loss of fifty-nine jobs. This was the last creamery in the dale. The philistines at Dairy Crest transferred production of Wensleydale cheese to Lancashire. Six months later there was a management buyout led by local businessman John Gibson. With the help of eleven members of the former workforce, cheese making was revived in Wensleydale. In 2015 it employed over 200 locals and bought from 36 farms in Wensleydale. It has a turnover of £27m and contributes £12m to the local economy.

111. The White Hart Country Inn, Hawes

Main Street, Hawes DL8 3QL
01969 667214
info@whitehartcountryinn.co.uk
www.whitehartcountryinn.co.uk

A 16th century coaching Inn.

If evidence were needed that Wensleydale is as English a cheese as Cheddar, then read on:

George Orwell, In his essay 'In Defence of English Cooking', rates Wensleydale as second only to Stilton among British cheeses.

Wensleydale was, of course, one of the cheeses listed by John Cleese in the Monty Python sketch 'The Cheese Shop' in 1972. What's more, the shop owner, played by Michael Palin, was called 'Henry Wensleydale', just to add to the confusion.

In the 1990s, sales of Wensleydale were in the doldrums, only to be rescued, quite by chance, by the Wallace and Gromit animated shorts *A Grand Day Out, The Wrong Trousers,* and *A Close Shave* when Wallace, a cheese aficionado, mentioned Wensleydale as his favourite. The company contacted Aardman Animations about a licence for a special brand of 'Wallace and Gromit Wensleydale', which proved to be an enormous success. When the 2005 full-length Wallace and Gromit film, *Curse of the Were-Rabbit*, was released, sales of Wensleydale cheeses increased by 23 per cent.

There were two other pubs in Hawes: the Black Bull, which closed in 1959 in Market Place; according to the Lost Pubs Project, 'At the last Brewster Sessions on 6th February 1959 no application was made to renew the licence on the grounds of structural deficiency. The last publican was Constance Mary Sharples. The publican in 1893 was Thomas Dinsdale'.

And Shaw Paddock Inn – the publican in 1871 was Richard Thwaite, in 1893 James Park.

Buttersett

Near Hawes. Also goes by the names of Burtersett and Butterside. Sir Edmund Hillary, the first man to climb Everest, is a direct descendant of John and Mary Hillary of Hillary Hall, Burtersett. The village water taps can still be seen; today, water is carried from the beck for two old cottages which are still occupied. The old candle mill survives – candles were made by William Metcalfe, who had the nickname 'Candle Willie'. Electricity was finally installed in 1951. 'Bump Knitting' is knitting with thick yarn as done by the women, to make stockings, jumpers and jackets.

Buttertubs Pass

Also near Hawes. Possibly named after potholes used by farmers to cool their butter in while resting on the way to market.

The *Dalesman* Salesman

A wonderful picture of a Dalesman 'sales meeting' at Buttertubs Pass. The man on the left is Mr P.A. Burt who was a close friend of the magazine's founder Harry Scott and did a lot of work for the company. Ron Hinson (husband of the photographer Lucie) is the man on the left.

© Lucie Hinson

Lucie Hinson at Buttertubs

© Lucie Hinson

The breathtaking pass runs from Simonstone towards Thwaite; the 20 metre deep fluted limestone potholes apparently got their name from when farmers would stop there on their way to market. During hot weather they would put the butter they were bringing into the potholes to keep it cool. The road is Jeremy Clarkson's favourite in Yorkshire; he describes it as 'England's only truly spectacular road', and he probably knows.

112. The Crown Inn, Askrigg

Main Street, Askrigg DL8 3HQ
01969 650298
www.thecrowninnaskrigg.jimdo.com

Askrigg was the first village in Yorkshire to be lit by electricity. Askrigg is Old Norse, made up of a combination of askr, ash tree and hryggr, ridge: the ridge where ash trees grew, which tells us that the village was settled

by Vikings. The oldest settlement probably dates back to the Iron Age. In 1066 the manor was held by Arnketil. Clock-making and the knitting of hosiery were once the industries here. 'Drunken Barnaby,' whose *Journeyings* were published in 1638, wrote: 'Thence to Askrigg, market noted, But no handsomeness about it. Neither magistrate nor mayor Ever were elected there. Here poor people live by knitting, To their trading, breeding fitting.'

113. The Kings Arms, Askrigg

Main Street, Askrigg DL8 3HQ
01969 650113
www.kingsarmsaskrigg.co.uk

An 18th century coaching inn that starred as the Drovers in TV's *All Creatures Great and Small.*

A John Pratt built this in 1767 as a manor house and stables. A racing man, Pratt was a jockey at Newmarket while his filly, Imperatrix, won the St Leger in 1782. His Mare Phoenix gave its name to another pub in the village. The house became a coaching inn from 1800.

114. The White Rose, Askrigg

Main Street, Askrigg, Leyburn, North Yorkshire DL8 3HG
01969 650515
stay@thewhiterosehotelaskrigg.co.uk
www.thewhiterosehotelaskrigg.co.uk

A former 19th century residence, the former Winville Hotel offers Yorkshire Dales Askrigg Ale from the nearby brewery. There was also a Queens Arms here; the publican in 1893 was Margaret Trotter.

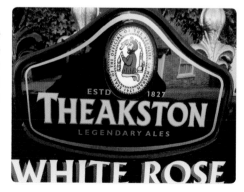

115. Victoria Arms Inn, Worton

Worton, Bainbridge DL8 3EU
01969 650314

The Victoria Arms public house from 1698 had one of the longest serving landlords in British pub history. Ralph Daykin was the publican at the Victoria Arms between 1956 and 2013.

What?ub describes this quirky pub best:

> *There is nowhere else quite like the Victoria. The bar is unchanged for many decades and the pub is a treasure trove of decorations that include ultra-violet lighting in the games room, a sign to 'Bedrooms 50–70' and the back half of a fox. Beware of everything and anything – you never know quite what might happen.*

The Guardian is more graphic:

> *The classic front-room pub, run by landlord Ralph Daykin since 1956, serves Black Sheep Riggwelter Ale next to the rear end of a stuffed fox, pimped with a water pump. At judicious moments, it lifts its tail and 'pees' on surprised customers.*

(Ian Belcher in *The Guardian*, 11 April 2009)

The name Worton means the herb or vegetable garden (Old English wyrt-tun). Werton in the Domesday Book.

116. The Rose & Crown Hotel, Bainbridge

Bainbridge DL8 3EE
01969 650225
info@theprideofwensleydale.co.uk
www.theprideofwensleydale.co.uk

An extremely ancient pub: this large whitewashed building on the village green claims to go back to 1445. It boasts a low-beamed stone flagged bar. The forest horn in the reception hall is a replacement and recalls the fact that in centuries past Wensleydale was a dense forest and Bainbridge was a safe haven for the foresters that worked in it. The horn was blown to guide the foresters safely home. Today it is sounded every night at 10 p.m. from the Feast of Holy Rood (27 September) to Shrove Tuesday. The original horn is in Bolton Castle.

In 1500 there were fun and games in Bainbridge: the parish register records that 'the housewives of Bainbridge were tippling on the Sabbath in the Rose and Crown instead of attending Divine Service'.

Bainbridge simply means the bridge over the River Bain. Bainbridge, Roman Virosidum, is notable for the remains of a Roman fort, which can be found east of Bainbridge on Brough Hill. Nearby is Cam High Road, which follows the line of a Roman road. The Rose and Crown is one of Yorkshire's oldest pubs, serving since 1445. The River Bain is officially a Main River, and is, therefore, at around two and a half miles long, the shortest river in England.

117. George and Dragon Inn, Aysgarth

Aysgarth, Leyburn North Yorkshire DL8 3AD
01969 663358
info@georgeanddragonaysgarth.co.uk
www.georgeanddragonaysgarth.co.uk

Less than a mile from the breathtaking Aysgarth falls, this was a 17th century coaching inn. The name Aysgarth means a gap in the hills where oak trees grew. The village is mentioned in the Domesday Book as Echescard. Aysgarth is derived from the Old Norse words eiki, meaning oak, and skarð, meaning open space. The famous Falls are a spectacular triple flight of waterfalls on the Ure over a one-mile stretch. Ruskin, Turner and Wordsworth painted or composed poetry here with the Falls as their subject.

118. Aysgarth Falls Hotel, Aysgarth (formerly the Palmer Flatt Hotel)

Aysgarth Falls Hotel, Aysgarth, Leyburn, North Yorkshire DL8 3SR
01969 663775 or 07972 273222
info@aysgarthfallshotel.com
www. aysgarthfallshotel.com

The original name of this hotel derives from its position on the site of a medieval hospital where ill pilgrims returning from the Holy Land Crusades were treated. These patients often carried palm leaves back with them as mementoes and as symbols of their pilgrimage – and so became known as 'palmers'. The existing building dates from the 18th century and in 1854 was described as 'a wayside hostelry of truly rural appearance, but possessing excellent accommodation and liquors, for the numerous parties of visitors to the Falls, by whom it is much frequented in the summer months'. The current owners have, sadly, renamed the pub the dull and 'commercially correct' Aysgarth Falls Hotel – devoid of and stripped of any history.

119. The Wheatsheaf, Carperby

Main Street, Carperby, Leyburn DL8 4DF
01969 663216
info@wheatsheafinwensleydale.co.uk
www.wheatsheafinwensleydale.co.uk

One mile north of Aysgarth Falls. The inn dates from the early 1800s when it doubled as the coaching inn and the village butchers. Alf Wight (of James Herriot fame) spent his honeymoon here, as did his bride presumably. Greta Garbo stayed after a performance entertaining troops at Catterick Camp with Henry Hall in January 1942.

Carper is an Old Irish personal name, Caipere, meaning charioteer. By is the Viking word for a settlement leading us to believe that the founder of this place was of mixed Irish Viking origin. In the 17th century the village was a hotbed of Quakerism: its largest building is still today the Friends' Meeting House built in 1864. The name of the Wheatsheaf betrays important corn growing at some time in the past.

120. The George Inn, Thoralby

Thoralby, Leyburn, North Yorkshire DL8 3SU
01969 663256
thegeorgeinn@thoralby.com
www.thegeorgeinnthoralby.com

The pub was built in 1732. The village name means Thorold's farm (Old Norse personal name Thoraldr + Old Norse). Toresbi and Turoldesbi in the Domesday Book. After the Norman invasion the lands were awarded to Count Alan of Brittany, who granted the local manor to Bernwulf, who had held the manor before this. The manor was eventually acquired by the lords of Middleham until the Middleham manor holdings were sold piecemeal by commissioners of the Crown in the mid-17th century. There are twenty-six Grade II listed buildings in the village, which include the old chapel, post office and public house.

121. Bolton Arms Inn, Redmire

Redmire DL8 4EA
01969 624336
info@boltonarmsredmire.co.uk
www.boltonarmsredmire.co.uk

Redmire means the pool covered with reeds. Redmire is at the terminus of the Wensleydale Railway.

122. Fox & Hounds, West Burton

Leyburn DL8 4JY
01969 663111
the.fox.hounds2@gmail.com
www.foxandhoundswestburton.co.uk

The village has its own hidden waterfalls which are surely one of the most popular subjects for photographers coming to Wensleydale and in summer provide the most perfect swimming pool for locals and holidaymakers alike.

(from the website)

The small waterfall with the remains of the town mill is known as Cauldron Falls because of the beautiful plunge pool, and was painted by Turner. The Black Bull here closed in the 1960s.

123. Street Head Inn, Newbiggin

Newbiggin in Bishopsdale, Leyburn DL8 3TE
01969 663282
thestreeheadinn@gmail.com
www.thestreetheadinn.co.uk

The Street Head Inn is a Grade II listed Yorkshire Dales free house dating from the 1700s; this coaching inn has been welcoming travellers for nearly 300 years. The name means the new building or outhouse (Old English + Middle English) in Bishopdale. In 1228 it was known as the very German-sounding Neubigging. There is another Newbiggin just seven miles away near Askrigg.

124. The Wensleydale Heifer, West Witton

Leyburn, North Yorkshire DL8 4LS
01969 622 322
info@wensleydaleheifer.co.uk
https://www.wensleydaleheifer.co.uk/reply2.php

With regard to the pub's name, the Wensleydale Heifer was one of many bulls in Yorkshire. Others include: The Castle Howard Ox (York); The Blackwell Ox (Carlton and Sutton-on-the-Forest now closed); The Airedale Heifer (Mirfield) and The Craven Heifer (Heckmondwike, Ilkley, Stainforth, Barnoldswick and Skipton). Then there is The Chained Bull at Moortown, Leeds and the Durham Ox in Crayke – Durham because Crayke was in the Bishopric of Durham.

West Witton was originally known just as Witton, and was mentioned (as Witun) in the Doomsday Book. The name is Old English, from widu and tūn, meaning 'wood settlement', probably a place where wood was felled. By the late 12th century, the village became known as West Witton to distinguish it from East Witton, five miles down Wensleydale.

The village is renowned for its 'Burning of Bartle' ceremony held on the Saturday nearest 24 August, St Bartholomew's Day. A larger-than-life effigy of 'Bartle' is paraded around the village, displaying glowing eyes. Bartle stops at various strategic places to recite this doggerel, before finally being burnt at Grassgill End to much merry singing.

> On Penhill Crags he tore his rags; Hunter's Thorn he blew his horn;
> Capplebank Stee happened a misfortune and brak' his knee; Grisgill Beck
> he brak' his neck; Wadham's End he couldn't fend; Grassgill End we'll
> mak' his end. Shout, lads, shout.

The Star Inn here closed in the 1970s; the publican in 1893 was Mrs Edward Graham.

125. The White Swan Hotel, Middleham

Market Place, Middleham DL8 4PE
01969 622093
enquiries@whiteswanhotel.co.uk
www.whiteswanhotel.co.uk

Middleham is an Anglo-Saxon name meaning middle village. It was recorded in the Domesday Book as 'Medelai'. Building of Middleham Castle began in 1119; it was later known as the 'Windsor of the North'. Richard, Duke of Gloucester (the future Richard III) came here to learn how to be a knight in 1462. Edward IV and Henry VI were held prisoner here during the Wars of the Roses. Richard, Duke of Gloucester became master of the castle in 1471 and used the castle as his political base as he administered the North for his brother Edward IV under the Council of the North. Richard married Anne Neville, in 1472; their son Edward was born here (c. 1473) and here is where he died in April 1484. Richard III died in August 1485 in the Battle of Bosworth – the last reigning monarch to die on the battlefield.

126. The Black Bull, Middleham

Market Place, Middleham DL8 4NX
01969 624792
info@theblackbullmiddleham.co.uk

127. Dante (former Black Swan Inn), Middleham

Market Place, Middleham DL8 4NP
01969 622221

128. Richard III Hotel, Middleham

Market Place, Middleham DL8 4NP
01969 624987
www.richard111hotel.com

Richard III (1452–1485) was King of England from 1483 until his death at the Battle of Bosworth Field. Richard spent some years during his childhood from 1461 until 1465 at Middleham Castle, under the tutelage of his cousin Richard Neville, 16th Earl of Warwick (later known as the 'Kingmaker'), who took responsibility for his knightly training.

129. Sandpiper Inn, Leyburn

Market Place, Leyburn DL8 5AT
01969 622206
hsandpiper99@aol.com
https://www.sandpiperinn.co.uk/

Leborne in the Domesday Book. The name is derived from 'Ley' or 'Le' (clearing), and 'burn' (stream), meaning clearing by the stream. Leyburn is linked to Middleham, two miles away, by one of the most unusual river bridges in England, built in 1829 as one of the first examples of a suspension bridge. Turner passed through Leyburn in September 1816 during his tour of Yorkshire to make sketches for a series of watercolours to illustrate *A General History of the County of York* by Thomas Dunham Whitaker. Mary Queen of Scots was reputedly recaptured on the Shawl above the village after her escape from Bolton Castle *en route* to Fotheringay.

130. The Leyburn Bolton Arms, Leyburn

Market Place, Leyburn DL8 5BW
01969 623327
info@theleyburnboltonarms.co.uk
www.theleyburnboltonarms.com

Named after Bolton Castle to the north-west. The castle was built between 1378 and 1399 by Richard, 1st Baron Scrope of Bolton, and is an example of a quadrangular castle. In 1536 John, 8th Baron Scrope backed the Pilgrimage of Grace against the religious reforms of King Henry VIII and gave Adam Sedbar, Abbot of Jervaulx sanctuary in the castle. In consequence, John Scrope had to flee to Skipton pursued by the King's men but Abbot Sedbar was caught and executed. In retribution, the king ordered Bolton castle to be torched, causing extensive damage.

Mary, Queen of Scots stayed at Bolton for six months, from July 1568. After her defeat in Scotland at the Battle of Langside in 1568 she fled to England, thus posing a threat to Protestant Queen Elizabeth I. Mary was given Henry Scrope's own apartments in the South-West tower. Of her retinue of fifty-one knights, servants and ladies-in-waiting only thirty of her men and six ladies-in-waiting were able to stay in the castle, the rest taking lodgings nearby. Her household included cooks, grooms, hairdresser, embroiderer, apothecary, physician and surgeon. Bolton Castle was not really suitable for housing a queen, so tapestries, rugs and furniture were borrowed from local houses and nearby Barnard Castle. Queen Elizabeth herself loaned some pewter vessels as well as a copper kettle. In January 1569 Mary left Bolton Castle and was taken to Tutbury in Staffordshire where she spent much of the eighteen years before her execution in 1587.

131. The Golden Lion, Leyburn

Market Place, Leyburn DL8 5AS
01969 622161
goldenlionhotelleyburn@yahoo.co.uk
www.goldenlionleyburn.co.uk

132. The Pheasant Inn, Harmby

Harmby, Leyburn DL8 5PA
01969 622223

The waterfall here is opposite the pub.

133. Old Horn Inn, Spennithorne

Leyburn DL8 5PR
01969 622370

A spen (Anglo Saxon) or spenni was a type of hedge and features in High Spen and Spennymoor in County Durham as well as in Spennithorne. We hear of foxes jumping twice over 'a spenne' leading to the belief that a spen was a hedge or something like a hedge. There may also be a link to the Anglo-Saxon 'spannan' meaning to fasten or the Old High German spanan meaning to entice. Spennithorne was recorded in the Domesday Book as Speningetorp and later as Spenithorn in 1150, Spennigthorn in 1289 and Spenythorne in 1285. The thorne in Spennithorne, probably denotes a thorn tree, although the early spelling 'torp' could be 'thorpe' the Danish word for a small farm. The Spen valley in west Yorkshire is another place containing the name spen.

134. The Blue Lion, East Witton

East Witton, Nr Leyburn, North Yorkshire DL8 4SNT
01969 624273
enquiries@thebluelion.co.uk
http://www.thebluelion.co.uk/

135. The Cover Bridge Inn, East Witton

East Witton, Nr Leyburn, North Yorkshire DL8 4SQ
01969 623250
enquiries@thecoverbridgeinn.co.uk
www.thecoverbridgeinn.co.uk

The Cover Bridge Inn (formerly called the Forresters Arms and before that the Masons Arms), is alongside the River Cover, a few hundred yards upstream from the confluence with the River Ure. The pub's oldest part was probably built around 1670, to cater for the increasing trade on the drovers' route from Coverdale – the ancient road from Richmond and the North crossed the River Ure and then continued up Coverdale. This was also the monk road from Jervaux Abbey to Middleham.

The pub is famous for two good reasons: it was where monks took refuge during the destruction of Jervaulx Abbey in the Reformation: not only did they enjoy a pint or two of ale but they kept alive the recipe of Wensleydale cheese. It was also where the first formally recorded game of cricket took place in 1706. The 300th anniversary was celebrated In 2006 in grand style with a festival of cricket and a flypast by the Red Arrows and a Spitfire and Hurricane with musical accompaniment provided by the band of the Royal Regiment of Fusiliers.

THE GUEST PUB

136. The Old Bell Tavern, Harrogate

6 Royal Parade, Harrogate HG1 2SZ
01423 507930
http://www.markettowntaverns.co.uk/

The tavern's name refers to the fact that until 1815 an earlier inn, The Bell, occupied the site. The original Bell Tavern was one of the early 17th century alehouses which served visitors to Harrogate's world famous Old Sulphur Well which lies beneath the dome of the Pump Room museum opposite.

It was sometimes called the 'Blue Bell', because of the colour of its sign; the inn was also a stage in the York to Harrogate coaching journey; the 'machine' had its York terminus at the Black Swan in Peasholme Green there arriving 'in time for dinner'.

The Bell tavern closed in November 1815, after which the property was a private residence until 1846 when the site was cleared for the building of Royal Parade; the original Bell's cellars were incorporated into the new building. A set of historic drawings showing the original Bell Inn are on display in the Old Bell bar lobby area.

In 1786, the tenants of the original Bell reputedly 'provided a stock of the best wines and other liquors, and furnished the house in a manner commodious for the reception of the genteelest families ...'

In November 2001 the ground floor of No. 7 Royal Parade was incorporated into the tavern. This was originally the world famous Farrah's Harrogate Toffee shop: the room has been restored to its former glory with the centrepiece comprising the original Farrah shop display unit – a veritable museum of Farrah memorabilia.

Part of the Farrah Toffee display

Harrogate Toffee was invented by confectioner Robert Swan in 1847. Robert left the recipe to his assistant Ann Farrah whose husband Joseph continued the business until he died in 1897 and his son John became the owner. In 1897 the company was established and adopted the Farrah trade mark. John Farrah's shop was originally on Royal Parade but closed in the mid-1990s and now stands on Montpellier Parade.

The aim, and the unique selling point, of the top-selling Original Harrogate Toffee, was to cleanse the palate of the putrid taste of Harrogate's sulphur water. Original Harrogate Toffee is similar to both butterscotch and barley sugar and uses three different types of sugar, butter and lemon to give a unique texture and flavour. It is still made in copper pans and packaged in the recognisable trade-mark blue and silver embossed tins.

According to a newspaper clipping on the wall, former US President Bill Clinton visited the pub during a trip to Britain: he downed a Diet Pepsi.

DALES BREWERIES

Some of the breweries that serve pubs in the National Park.

Black Sheep Brewery, Masham

The Black Sheep Brewery, Wellgarth, Masham, North Yorkshire HG4 4EN
01765 689227
reception@blacksheep.co.uk
www.blacksheepbrewery.com

The Black Sheep Brewery grew out of Paul Theakston's ambition to create a new but traditional style brewery in Masham after the six-generation family firm of T. & R. Theakston's was bought by Matthew Brown and then Scottish & Newcastle Breweries in 1987. Paul bought the North Yorkshire Maltings Company, originally part of the former Lightfoot's brewery site, from an animal feed company.

October 1992 first saw Black Sheep beers served in pubs in and around the Yorkshire Dales. Riggwelter is one of their popular beers and takes its name from the dialect words for a sheep that is on its back and struggling to get up – riggwelted. This, in turn, is derived from the old Viking words for rigg meaning back and velte to overturn. Riggwelter is also popular in Sweden, being in the top twenty of bottled ales sold there. The brewery now produces over 75,000 barrels a year.

A Black Sheep brewery tour

Daleside Brewery, Harrogate

Camwal Road, Harrogate HG1 4PT
01423 880022
enquiries@dalesidebrewery.com
www. dalesidebrewery.com

Established in the mid-1980s by a family with a brewing heritage stretching back more than 600 years, Daleside moved to their present premises in Starbeck in 1992. Beers include the award-winning Morocco Ale, Old Legover, Ripon Jewel, and Monkey Wrench; export markets include the USA, Canada, Australia, Denmark, Sweden and Spain. Morocco Ale was chosen as the beer to accompany the lamb main course at the All Party Beer Group, Annual Dinner, at the House of Commons in July 2015.

Craig Witty: the head brewer cleaning the copper. Sketch © Colin Graham.

Skimming the yeast. Sketch © Colin Graham.

Dark Horse Brewery, Hetton

Coonlands Laithe, Hetton, Skipton, North Yorkshire BD23 6LY
01756 730555
richard@darkhorsebrewery.co.uk
http://www.darkhorsebrewery.co.uk/

Dent Brewery Ltd

Cowgill, Dent LA10 5TQ
01539 625326
laptop@dentbrewery.co.uk
www.dentbrewery.co.uk

Dent Brewery has been crafting ales for around 30 years; it is one of the most remote breweries in the England. The Brewery Tap is The George & Dragon in Dent village.

Hambleton Ales, Melmerby

Melmerby Green Road, Melmerby, Ripon HG4 5NB
01765 640108
office@hambletonales.co.uk
www.hambletonales.co.uk

Established in 1991 in the hamlet of Holme on Swale. From the website:

Armed with nothing more than a pair of wellies, some old steel tanks and a rusty Peugeot 205, Nick [Stafford] built his brewery with blood, sweat and tears at the bottom of his in-laws' garden … Why did he do this? Simply because he wanted to make great beer …

Today demand has meant that we have moved out of the garden, and we also have slightly shinier tanks, but Nick's original ambition still stands.

Kirkby Lonsdale Brewery

015242 72221 Royal Barn: 015242 71918
info@kirkbylonsdalebrewery.com
http://www.kirkbylonsdalebrewery.com/

From the website:

Established in 2009, we are a family run business whose main objective has been to bring back the art of brewing to the centre of Kirkby Lonsdale. Nine years, 33 different beers and a huge dose of hard work later we have established two brewing sites and a tap house to showcase our brewing team and their creations. Each beer we brew is named or linked to an aspect of the town and its history.

Mithril Ales, Richmond

Aldbrough St John, Richmond, North Yorkshire DL11 7TL
01325 374817

Pennine Brewing Co, Well

Well Hall Farm, Well, Bedale, North
Yorkshire DL8 2PX
01677 470111
info@pennine-brewing.co.uk
www. pennine-brewing.co.uk

Set up in 2013, Pennine were one of
the first brewers in the UK to put the
units of alcohol per pint on their pump
clips.

A Pennine Brewing stand at
Pontefract in 2015

Recoil Brewing Company, Clitheroe

Units 9–10, Lincoln Park, Salthill Industrial Estate, Clitheroe, Lancashire BB7 1QD
01200 613777
info@recoilbrewing.com
www.recoilbrewing.co/

Richmond Brewing Company

The Station Yard, Richmond DL10 4LD
01748 828266
enquiries@richmondbrewing.co.uk
www.richmondbrewing.co.uk

Roosters Brewery, Knaresborough

Wetherby Road, Knaresborough HG5 8LJ
01423 865959
http://www.roosters.co.uk/

Roosters started life in 1980 as Franklins Brewery based
at the Gardeners Arms in Harrogate. Two years later, Sean
Franklin moved the company with a new name: Roosters.
The name was inspired by John Wayne and his role as
Rooster Cogburn in *True Grit* leading to the launch of

Roosters brewing plant

Yankee and other western themed brands. Since 2011, it has been run by the Fozard family in Knaresborough.

Outlaw is a subsidiary company run for specialist and trial beers. Under Outlaw, the Fozards produce a coffee porter in conjunction with Betty and Taylor's of Harrogate; Bettys are also involved in a jasmine tea beer.

T&R Theakston Ltd, Masham

01765 680 000
info@theakstons.co.uk
www.theakstons.co.uk

The sixteenth largest brewer in the UK by market share, and the second largest brewer under family ownership after Shepherd Neame. It was founded in 1827 by Robert Theakston and John Wood at The Black Bull pub and brewhouse in Masham. By 1875, control of the brewery Theakston passed to his son Thomas who increased the size of the company when he built the new brewery on the Paradise Fields. In 1919 the company acquired and closed down the Lightfoot Brewery in Masham.

Paul Theakston who had been Managing Director since 1968 left Theakston's in 1988, and set up the Black Sheep Brewery in the old Lightfoot Brewery premises – next to the White Bear Hotel, a Theakston pub. Old Peculier (5.6 per cent ABV) is Theakston's most celebrated beer, made under this name since the 1890s. It gets its name from the peculier of Masham, a peculier being a parish outside the jurisdiction of a diocese. In 1985 *The Economist* called it the 'doyen of real ales'.

Three Peaks Brewery, Settle

7 Craven Terrace, Settle, Yorkshire BD24 9DB
01729 822939

Thwaites, Blackburn

Daniel Thwaites PLC, Penny Street, Blackburn, Lancashire BB1 6HL
01254 686868
info@thwaites.co.uk
www.thwaites.co.uk

Thwaites Brewery was founded in 1807 by Daniel Thwaites in Blackburn. Thwaites only sells to its own estate of pubs, inns and hotels. The company has over 270 pubs, mainly in the North of England.

Timothy Taylor, Keighley

Knowle Spring Brewery, Keighley,
West Yorkshire BD21 1AW
01535 603139
tim@timtaylors.co.uk
www.timothytaylor.co.uk

Timothy Taylor's is a family-owned brewery founded in 1858 by Timothy Taylor. Timothy Taylor's best known ale is Landlord, a pale ale that was created for miners, to compete against local rival Barnsley Bitter. The brand grew in popularity in 2003 when Madonna said in an interview that it was her favourite beer. In 2015, Timothy Taylor's bought The Devonshire Hotel in Grassington.

Wall's Brewery, Northallerton

1 Binks Close, Standard Way Business Park, Northallerton, North Yorkshire DL6 2YB
01609 258226
david.wall@wallsbrewery.co.uk

Wensleydale Brewery, Leyburn

Unit 4, Badger Court, Harmby Road, Leyburn, North Yorkshire DL8 5BF
01969 622463
enquiries@wensleydalebrewery.co.uk
http://www.wensleydalebrewery.co.uk/

Wensleydale Brewery was first opened in 2003 at The Foresters Arms in Carlton.

Wharfedale Brewery, Ilkley

The Back Barn, 16 Church Street, Ilkley, West Yorkshire LS29 9DS
01943 609587
info@wharfedalebrewery.com
http://www.wharfedalebrewery.com/

This Wharfedale Brewery is in Ilkley in Wharfedale; it is the third Wharfedale Brewery: the two previous breweries were in Wetherby from 1756 and in Hetton near Grassington opened by the Duke of Kent in 2003. During World War I Wharfedale Brewery in Wetherby was requisitioned to billet troops, and then taken

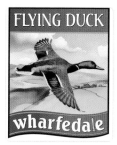

over by Oxleys mineral water company. In 1943 it was used to make Coca-Cola for the many American troops in the area.

The latest Wharfedale Brewery, the Ilkley version, was created in 2012 by sixteen real ale enthusiasts, many of whom are former chairmen of Ilkley & District Round Table and founder members of the Ilkley Beer Festival in 2008.

They redeveloped the former Mallard Inn (more recently the Albert) on Church Street, a Grade II listed property built in 1709. The pub, which is one of Ilkley's oldest buildings and is noted in Pevsner's *Buildings of England* for its architectural importance, was renamed the Flying Duck: a microbrewery was incorporated into a barn at the back.

In May 2014 Wharfedale Brewery launched 'The Ales Way' – Wharfedale's Ale Trail, which encompasses fifteen pubs throughout Wharfedale between Ilkley and Hubberholme. Every time you visit an Ales Way pub and buy a pint of Wharfedale Brewery beer you get a stamp in your souvenir card. Once you've got enough stamps the souvenir card can be exchanged for a t-shirt and brewery presentation pack.

Yorkshire Dales Brewery, Askrigg

Abbey Works, Askrigg, Leyburn DL8 3BJ
01969 622027

The best brewery in Askrigg.

TEMPERANCE

It seems only right, in a book that celebrates the English pub, to remember that not everyone in the nation has always been enamoured by pubs, inns, taverns and alehouses. Indeed, some eschew such establishments completely and, for various good reasons, avoid beer and other alcoholic beverages. To provide a degree of context and balance, it is important we look at temperance and abstinence.

The earliest temperance societies were inspired by Belfast professor of theology, and Presbyterian Church of Ireland minister John Edgar, who famously poured his stash of whisky out of his window in 1829. Joseph Livesey underwrote his philanthropic work in temperance with the profits he made from cheese production. The word teetotal comes from a stuttering speech by Richard (Dickie) Turner, a follower of Livesey, in Preston in 1833: 'I'll be reet down out-and-out t-t-total for ever and ever.'

Livesey opened the first temperance hotel in 1833 and the next year founded the first temperance magazine, *The Preston Temperance Advocate* (1834–1837). The British Association for the Promotion of Temperance was established by 1835 and had as its mission statement 'Education for all'. A contemporary pamphlet urges residents to 'come as you are, do not stoop to black your boots'.

In 1847, the Band of Hope was founded in Leeds, the aim of which was saving working class children from the perils of drink. The members were obliged to pledge to abstain 'from all liquors of an intoxicating quality, whether ale, porter, wine or ardent spirits, except as medicine'.

In 1853, the Maine law in the US inspired the United Kingdom Alliance – a hardline group of prohibitionists – to advocate, divisively, a similar law prohibiting the sale of alcohol in the UK. This was opposed by less radical temperance organisations who preferred moral persuasion to a legal ban. The impotence of legislation in this field became all too clear when the Sale of Beer Act 1854, which restricted Sunday opening hours, had to be repealed, following widespread rioting. In 1859 a prototype prohibition bill was overwhelmingly defeated in the House of Commons.

A breakthrough came in the shape of Norman Shanks Kerr who promoted the treatment of inebriates and held that inebriety was a disease, not a vice. In 1884, in response to the inadequacy of the Habitual Drunkards Act of 1879, he founded the Society for the Study and Cure of Inebriety and was the first president; the society still exists as the Society for the Study of Addiction.

Secular temperance organisations connected to the Labour movement started to emerge, for example the Scottish Prohibition Party, founded by a communist temperance activist called Bob Stewart – a Marxist offshoot called the Prohibition and Reform Party, which later became part of the Communist Party of Great Britain in 1920.

The former Manchester City FC football stadium, Maine Road, gets its name from a renaming of Dog Kennel Lane by members of the Temperance Movement, inspired by the 1853 Maine law.

Religion played a part: various Nonconformist groups – the Methodists, Quakers and The Salvation Army (founded 1864), lobbied Parliament to restrict alcohol sales.

In Wales, Lady Llanover, motivated by Calvinistic Methodists teachings, closed all the public houses on her estate and was an outspoken critic of the evil drink. The Church of England Temperance Society was founded in 1862; its volunteers in the court system led to the first probation service. The League of the Cross was a Catholic total abstinence organisation founded in 1873 by Cardinal Manning. In 1876 the British Women's Temperance Association was formed to persuade men to stop drinking, rebranded in 2006 as the White Ribbon Association.

The battle for temperance, then, was hard fought; it may be that those who fought the fight believed that if only one drinker was dissuaded from the drink then the arduous fight was well worth it. In the event, it is estimated that in 1900 10 per cent of the adult population was teetotal. That must be considered a success. At the same time, we know that beer drinking was on the decline with 138 pubs calling time for the last time.

The pub was not helped by World War I, during which it was standard practice for (mainly male) workers in restricted occupations to have a drink before work and in the lunch break. This had a detrimental effect on productivity, particularly in munitions; so bad was it that David Lloyd George said in February 1915 when querying the reasons behind the shortfall in output: 'let us be perfectly candid. It is mostly the lure of the drink ... drink is doing more damage in the war than all the German submarines put together'. Duty on alcoholic beverages was raised, shorter opening hours were imposed, and alcoholic drinks were watered down. These measures had the desired effect: pubs closed in their droves. In 1931 a Royal Commission was able to declare that getting drunk had gone out of fashion; in modern parlance, it was no longer cool.

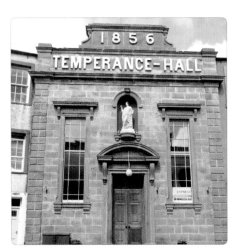

The imposing 1856 Temperance Hall in Kirkby Stephen in 2018

So, in passing the Defence of the Realm Act in 1914 the Liberal Government gave temperance an unexpected boost: pub hours were reduced, beer was watered down and was subject to a penny a pint extra tax; the momentum was maintained by the subsequent State Management Scheme in 1916, which nationalised breweries and pubs in certain areas of Britain where armaments manufacture was taking place.

The Cross Keys Temperance Inn, Cautley

Cautley, Sedbergh, Cumbria LA10 5NE
015396 20284
clowes@freeuk.com
http://www.cautleyspout.co.uk/

The Cross Keys Temperance Inn near Cautley Spout on the A683 north of Sedbergh – not really an inn then.

The Cross Keys first makes the record books when a Thomas Bland was living there in 1619; however, the building is late 16th century, extended in the early 18th century, and at the other end in the 19th century. The oldest part of the building is the parlour and the room above. In 1949 it was left to the National Trust in the will of Mrs Edith Adelaide Bunney, to be held as an unlicensed inn, in memory of her sister Miss Mary Blanche Hewetson.

Before it was an inn, in the early 1800s the Cross Keys was a farmhouse called High Haygarth, becoming an inn after 1819 when the Cautley road, which originally ran up over the Bluecaster Fell, was re-aligned to run on a more level route in front of High Haygarth.

The initials and 1730 date above the front door refer to John and Agnes Howgill who owned High Haygarth at that time.

After one rumbustious evening at the Cross Keys a relative of a local family by the name of Buck was being helped home towards Ravenstonedale by the then landlord. It would seem that this relative fell down the river bank at which the landlord tried to help him but only succeeded in falling into the River Rawthey where he drowned. On 27 October 1902 the Cross Keys was sold by auction at the Bull Hotel, Sedbergh, for £900.00 to Mrs Sarah Buck of Ravenstonedale. Mrs Buck re-sold it to Mrs Edith Adelaide Bunney who removed the liquor license, with the result that since 1902 the Cross Keys has been a Temperance Inn.

SOME STRANGE AND ECCENTRIC YORKSHIRE PUB NAMES

Some of Yorkshire's pub names are odd, arcane and obscure. Here are a few of the puzzling ones, in no particular order, although we might as well begin with The Puzzle Hall at Sowerby Bridge, which denotes the puzzles inside available to drinkers, which puzzled all. The Folly outside Halifax remembers the 270 feet high folly built by John E. Wainhouse to annoy his neighbour. The Salmon Leap (formerly The Station Hotel) at Sleights denotes the salmon leap on the River Esk there, while The Three Legs of Man in Leeds describes the Isle of Man coat of arms. Hull's Goat and Compasses is a corruption of the Puritan motto 'God encompasses us' while the city's Ravenser remembers the village on the Humber engulfed by the sea in 1346. Bell ringing is commemorated in The Ring of Bells in Barnsley. The nickname (Peter) of the landlady of The Just Peter Inn (once The Railway Inn) provides the name for this curious pub in Holme on Spalding Moor.

Between York and Malton is The Spitalbeck Inn, but there is no beck to be seen: the original inn was next to the Spital Beck a mile down the road at Barton Hill. In earlier times coaches would stop at the inn to collect two fresh horses to help the existing team haul its load to the top of the much steeper hill. Part of the building that became the inn was used as a hospital for Cromwellian soldiers during the siege at Scarborough Castle in the Civil War. Despite the image painted on its sign The Bruce Arms at West Tanfield has nothing to do with Robert the Bruce; it was originally named after the Bruce family, famous northern landowners. The Triangle Inn in Sowerby Bridge is vaguely mathematical, named as it is after the triangular piece of land on which the nearby village of Triangle is situated. In Triangle itself is The White Bear: the Triangle Cricket Club was founded at the pub as was the Triangle Reading Society; the pub was used as a Coroner's Court. Other White Bears prowl around Barnsley, Masham, Sowerby Bridge, Skircoat Green and, confusingly, Cow Green in Halifax. One bear that did no prowling was The Old White Beare at Norwood Green near Halifax from 1533: this pub was named after a ship that fought the Spanish Armada. There was a Leopard in York slain by the Luftwaffe in the 1942 Beideker raid; and one in Calverley (later The Thornhill Arms) dating back to 1673 and named after the three leopards on the coat of arms of the Weavers' Company. North of York, Haxby and the contiguous village of Wigginton are a veritable safari park with their Tiger, Red Lion and Black Horse. Another Tiger was in Hedon; there is a Blue Lion at East Witton. The Wolf in Luddenden, built in 1653, was said to be a rendezvous for army recruiting officers in the early 18th century; in 1745, Janet, a Scottish maid at the inn gave sanctuary to a soldier from Bonnie Prince Charlie's army who was being pursued by the English army. In 1877, the property was acquired by the Luddenden Co-operative Society; the Luddenden Working Men's Club & Institute was also here from 1880 until 1946.

Foxes abound, with or without the hounds; one Fox is in Holgate in York, another was in Low Petergate dating from the 15th century but demolished in 1958; its other names were The Lord Byron and The Beech Tree.

Here are some quintessentially Yorkshire-named Yorkshire pubs. The Wapping Spring brewery and the spring that watered it in Outlane just outside Huddersfield gave its name to The Wappy Spring Inn. The brewery closed in 1957. The Who Could A' Thowt It in Brighouse was the Masons' Arms until 1870. The Who Could A' Thowt It in Southowram was formerly Clough Head Cottage at Clough Head, Sunny Bank Lane and also known pithily as Who Would a Thowt It, Ba Gum Who'd A' Thowt It, and Ba Gum Who Wad A' Thowt It in the 1860s. There was a passage between the cellars of the pub and the cottage next door, which provided a quick escape for illegal drinkers. The pub closed in 1933; when it was demolished the stone and roof slates went into the rebuilding of Coventry after World War II. The Queen O'Towd Thatch at South Milford dates from 1720 and means nothing more than the queen with an old thatched roof – a feature that endured until the early 1900s. The Ram's Head at Denshaw was popularly known as T'Owd Tupps. The Needless got its name from the magistrate (depicted on the sign) who declared that another pub on the Morley–Batley road was 'needless' as there were already two. Needless prevailed, however, and became one of the many pubs in which Dick Turpin downed his last pint before incarceration. It was also called The Cardigan Arms. The Q in the Corner in Sheffield was famous for its blind fiddlers while The Warm Hearthstone nearby was well known for encouraging drinkers to dip their own bread into dripping from the pub's roasts. In Barnsley, The Gyngleboy is named after the slang term for a coin and later for someone who jingles coins in their pocket. The Tom Treddlehoyle at Pogmoor was local author Charles Roger's pen name. The uniquely titled 18th century Lettered Board is in Pickering on Smiddy Hill. The Samuel Plimsoll in Sheffield commemorates the man who saved many a seafarer's life when he did away with the 'coffin ships' and introduced his famous load line. Another life-saver is remembered by The Davy Lamp at Thrybergh near Rotherham. A male version of Knaresborough's Mother Shipton has been awarded eternal life in the sign of The Hermit Inn at Burley in Wharfedale (formerly The Woolpack): the hermit in question is the prophesying Job Senior – the bastard son of a wealthy Ilkey landowner born in 1780. Senior also had the special skill of being able to sing tenor, treble, alto and bass all in the same hymn. When his wife died, he was blamed and her relatives destroyed his house and stole all his money leaving him no choice but to become a hermit. The Henry Jenkins Inn at Kirby Malzeard remembers the man of that name who died in 1670 aged 169. The Floating Light stood on the scenic A62 over Standedge; it opened in 1940 and closed around 2000. The name derives from lights used by workers digging the canal tunnel – the longest in Britain – that runs beneath. The Nont Sarah's pub at Scammonden above Huddersfield is named after Aunt Sarah, the licensee some 150 years ago. At Ogden The Causeway Foot used to be known as The Buck Inn, The Goose Inn and The Peat Pitts in 1789 after the nearby peat pitts. The Naked Man Inn in Settle dates from 1663; it is happily matched with The Naked Woman one mile up the road in Langliffe dating from 1660. Less happily, both are long closed. The now shut Whale Fishery in York took its name from the licensee

Christopher Bean who was a harpooner on Hull boats in the Arctic and created a vivid sign representing a miniature carved whaling boat. The Leeds coaching inn The Bull and Mouth was a corruption of Boulogne Mouth popularised by Henry VIII when he captured Boulogne Harbour. The Feoffees (try saying it after a few pints) in Sheffield was built on the site of a 1726 poor school – feoffees being the term for the charitable trustees. The Old Silent at Stanbury near Haworth gets its name from the fact that Bonnie Prince Charlie hid there, and the locals maintained silence for a couple of weeks so that he could make good his escape.

In 1881 West Bottom Tavern in Halifax's Hob Lane was a row of three cottages for workers in the local quarries, the middle one of which was a beerhouse. The name was changed to The Hobbit after restoration in 1975. Also around Halifax T' Wheel Hoile was also known as Old Coley Mill Inn. It opened in 1830 and closed in the 1920s. The pub stood near Coley corn mill, which fell into disuse, leaving only the wheel hole once the dangerous mill wheel had been removed. The Whiskam Dandy was named after the hamlet of Whiskam Dandy. A less obvious railway hotel not called The Railway or The Station is the L. & Y.R. Hotel in Knottingley signifying the Lancashire and Yorkshire Railway. The Running Man in Halifax is a vivid reminder of the odious Halifax gibbet; freedom, and life, could be won by running a certain distance from the town. Failure, though, meant the gibbet after all and gave rise to the desperate refrain 'From Hull, Hell and Halifax, Good Lord Deliver Us'. There were four pubs called The New Delight around Halifax: one survives at Wanstalls; the name is taken from Milton's *Paradise Lost*: 'Heav'n's last best gift, my ever new delight' – Eve addressing Adam at Book V, 19. Once, it was called The Travellers' Rest. The Church Steps in Dewsbury is the only pub in Britain built on consecrated ground while The Postcard in Holmfirth is named after the comic post card firm, Balmforth, based there. The Flouch Inn from 1827 near Penistone is very odd: it was originally The New Inn but when the name was changed to The Plough, parts of the lettering, namely part of the p and part of the 'g', fell off …

Pubs named after local industry and the occupations they spawned are, of course, extremely common, and we have already seen a number of Yorkshire examples. Here is a small selection of the less usual, some are gone, some are still with us: Brassmoulders Arms (Leeds); Boatman's Rest (Barnsley); Brickmakers Arms (Hull); Butchers Arms (Batley); Carriers Arms (Morley); Clothiers Arms (Leeds); The Cobblers (Pontefract); Colliers Arms (Elland); Coopers Arms, Jolly Sailors, Miners and Millers Arms, Hammer and Stithy – a name for an anvil (Ossett); Engineers Arms (Hull); Electricians Hotel (Huddersfield); Fellmongers Arms (Leeds); Foresters Arms and Graziers Arms (Wakefeld); Horsebreakers Arms (Hutton Sessay); Jet Miners Arms (Great Broughton); Joiners Arms (Hampsthwaite); Nailmakers Arms (Sheffield); Ostlers Arms, Plasterers Arms and Skinners Arms (Leeds); Spinners Arms (Colne Bridge); Yarnspinners Arms (Bradford); Fishermans Hut (Leeds); Shepherd's Boy (Dewsbury); The Shears Inn (Hightown, Huddersfield). The Plummet Line in Halifax opened in 1898 and still retains its fine tiled nameplate. It is, of course, named after the builders' weighted line. Halifax can also boast The Pot O' Four – the pot used by wool combers to heat their combs. The Whisket in Todmorden was originally a beerhouse built by William Fielden – a basket-maker; a whisket is a name for a basket. The Collier at Elland recalls the boats that shipped the coal and not the men who dug it; the nearby Barge and Barrel evokes similar memories. The Slubbers Arms in Huddersfield gets its name from slubber, a person or machine that slubs, i.e. works carelessly – here, a reference to textile workers. The Veterinary Arms at Hunmanby is so named after the vet who supplemented his fees with the selling of ale.

There is nothing unusual about the name of The Globe at Raistrick; however, in 1910 the landlord hanged himself during the lunchtime session; his wife carried on serving until the session was over before she called the police. Less inviting pubs are: The World's End in Knaresborough – owned by Charles Blenkhorn, who also ran the nearby pleasure boats, hotel and café. He was also town postmaster; his sister was postmistress. At one time the pub sign is said to have depicted an earthquake with a bus falling into the River Nidd and the pub collapsing. The Cemetery Arms in Leeds and The Black Swan at Leyburn, which has a man-trap on the wall, are just as cheery. At South Kirby The Travellers doubled up as the village mortuary, as did the building next door to The Ship in Saltburn …

It comes as no surprise that beer, brewing and inns themselves feature frequently in pub names. There is a Cock and Bottle in York (formerly The Plumbers Arms and Duke's Place) and one in Skipton; The Corporation Brewery Taps in Doncaster, The Hogshead at Woodhouse near Sheffield and the amusing Jack and Gill in Allerton. You might have wanted to slip in the tiny Slip Inn north of York (now gone), although the pub of the same name on the city's Ouse refers to the river traffic; failing that, drop in at The Drop Inn in Guisely or go to The Local in Leeds for one of Hull's two Full Measures. Pig and Whistles (as in Pudsey) signify the mug into which your beer was poured from the jug (for example, in Leeds and the Falcon in Arncliffe). The Boy and Barrels at Selby and Mexborough is Bacchus, the Roman god of wine sitting on a tun of ale. The Hop Grove on Malton Road in York has been around since 1857 at least. Records refer to it under the name The Hop Pole Inn in 1889 and 1893.

CLOSING TIME

it'll all end in beers.

(Anon.)

'Laughing Len' knew all about closing time …

Ah we're drinking and we're dancing
And the band is really happening
And the Johnny Walker wisdom running high
And my very sweet companion
She's the angel of compassion
She's rubbing half the world against her thigh …
All the women tear their blouses off
And the men they dance on the polka-dots
And it's partner found, it's partner lost
And it's hell to pay when the fiddler stops
It's closing time …
And the place is dead as heaven on a Saturday night
And my very close companion
Gets me fumbling gets me laughing
She's a hundred but she's wearing
Something tight …
The whole damn place goes crazy twice
And it's once for the devil and once for Christ
But the boss don't like these dizzy heights
We're busted in the blinding lights
(Busted in the blinding lights)
Busted in the blinding lights
Of closing time

(Leonard Cohen (1934–2016), *Closing Time*)

For what it's worth here is my top eleven pubs in the Dales, in no particular order:

The Falcon, Arncliffe,
The Angel, Hetton
Barbon Inn, Barbon
The Buck, Buckden
The Black Horse, Giggleswick
Tan Hill Inn, near Reeth
The George, Hubberholme
The Sun Inn, Dent
The Craven Arms, Appletreewick
The Game Cock, Austwick
The Fountaine Inn, Linton

On the Arncliffe to Malham Road

Black Horse, Giggleswick; Tan Hall Inn, Miles from Nowhere; Sun Inn, Dent

Now ! – Will someone take me to a pub?

(G.K. Chesterton 1874–1936)

FURTHER READING

Brandon, D. *Discovering Pub Names and Signs*, Oxford, 2010.

Brandwood, G. *Licensed to Sell – The History and Heritage of the Public House*, 2nd edition, English Heritage, 2011.

Bruning, T. *Historic Pubs of England*, London, 2000.

Chrystal, P. *Tea: A Very British Beverage*, Stroud 2014.

Chrystal, P. *Coffee: A Drink for the Devil*, Stroud, 2016.

Chrystal, P. *Harrogate Pubs including Knaresborough*, Stroud, 2016.

Chrystal, P. *Hull Pubs*, Stroud, 2017.

Chrystal, P. *Old Yorkshire Country Life*, Catrine, 2017.

Chrystal, P. *The Place Names of Yorkshire, including Pub Names*, Catrine, 2017.

Chrystal, P. *Yorkshire Murders, Murders, Manslaughter, Madness & Executions*, Catrine, 2018.

Chrystal, P. *Pubs In & Around York*, 2018

Clark, P. *The English Alehouse: A Social History 1200–1830*, London, 1983.

Davis, B. *The Traditional English Pub: A Way of Drinking*, London, 1981.

Gamston, D. (ed.) *Yorkshire's Real Heritage Pubs: Pub Interiors of Special Historic Interest in Yorkshire and Humber*, CAMRA, St Albans, 2014.

Girouard, M. *Victorian Pubs*, Yale, 1984.

Gorham, M. *Back to the Local*, London, 2007.

Gorham, M. *Inside the Pub*, London, 1950.

Haydon, P. *The English Pub: A History*, London, 1994.

Long, P. *Hidden Inns of Yorkshire 2nd edition*, Aldermaston 2003.

Monckton, H.A. *A History of the English Public House*, London, 1969.

Monson-Fitzjohn, G.J. *Quaint Signs of Olde Inns*, London, 1926.

Oliver, B. *The Renaissance of the English Public House*, London 1947.

Pepper, B. *A Haunt of Rare Souls: The Old Inns and Pubs of Yorkshire*, Otley, 1990.

Priestley J.B. *The Other Place*, London 1953.

Priestley, J.B. *English Journey*, London, 1937.

Reid, M. *The Inn Way 2nd ed.*, Birmingham, 1997.

Scott Massie, I. *The Dale of Angels*, Hetton 2014, www.angelhetton.co.uk.

Swales, Bill, *The King's Head [Richmond]: A Brief History*, http://www.kingsheadrichmond.co.uk/wp-content/uploads/2018/05/Kings-Head-History-Booklet-2018.pdf.

Wainwright, A. *A Pennine Journey: The Story of a Long Walk in 1938*, London 1986.

https://pubheritage.camra.org.uk/home/home.asp?utm_medium=301&utm_source=heritagepubs.org.uk/home/home.asp

www.drinkaware.co.uk

www.yorkshire.camra.org.uk/

The Lost Pubs Project: www.closedpubs.co.uk

'The Landlord' by F.W. Elwell (1870–1958), in Ferens Art Gallery, Hull.

THE COUNTRYSIDE CODE

- Respect other people:

    consider the local community and other people enjoying the outdoors

    leave gates and property as you find them and follow paths unless wider access is available

- Protect the natural environment:

    leave no trace of your visit and take your litter home

    keep dogs under effective control

- Enjoy the outdoors:

    plan ahead and be prepared

    follow advice and local signs

Looking down Wharfedale towards Buckden.